Technology in Its Place

John F. LeBaron and Catherine Collier,
Editors

Sponsored by
The International Network
of Principals' Centers

Technology in Its Place

Successful Technology Infusion in Schools

JOSSEY-BASS
A Wiley Company
San Francisco

Jossey-Bass books and products are available through most bookstores. To contact Jossey-Bass directly, call (888) 378-2537, fax to (800) 605-2665, or visit our website at www.josseybass.com.

Substantial discounts on bulk quantities of Jossey-Bass books are available to corporations, professional associations, and other organizations. For details and discount information, contact the special sales department at Jossey-Bass.

Manufactured in the United States of America

Library of Congress Cataloging-in-Publication Data

Technology in its place : successful technology infusion in schools / John F. LeBaron, Catherine Collier, editors.
    p. cm.
  Includes index.
  ISBN 0-7879-5682-1 (alk. paper)
  1. Technological innovations. 2. Educational technology. I. LeBaron, John, date. II. Collier, Catherine. III. Title.
  T173.8 .T4238 2001
  371.33'4—dc21   00-012693

FIRST EDITION
PB Printing   10 9 8 7 6 5 4 3

For Anna
1908–2000

Contents

Preface

This is a book for educators concerned with the improvement of teaching and learning through technology. It offers a multifaceted vision of both the contribution that technology can make to effective schooling and the creative alignment of leadership and practice with theory and research. It examines practice from viewpoints ranging from global initiatives in international on-line learning to the local concerns of a single classroom. Written from the backdrop of educational reform, this book presents a comprehensive view of technology in schooling, addressing concerns of administration, strategic planning, curricular integration, and staff development.

The chapter authors offer successful track records of leadership and practice in the curricular integration of technology. Some of them are veteran contributors to this field. Others have more recently gained recognition for significant accomplishments in a rather short period of time. Each of them has a story to tell from practice, research, or a combination of the two. We hope that their stories add to the intellectual inventories of our readers as they seek to enhance learning and teaching with the unprecedented opportunities offered by technology.

Technology, Leadership, and the Curriculum

The successful infusion of technology into education depends on effective leadership and good sense about school culture. Leadership emerges from many different venues. This collection of perspectives is therefore aimed at the following groups:

- Teachers, higher education faculty, and professional developers
- School building and district administrators
- Technology coordinators and library media specialists
- Parents and community citizens
- Policymakers, elected and appointed
- Businesspeople and others in the private sector

Educational technology professional associations have accelerated dialogue with other leading groups of educators. For example, in cooperation with the U.S. Department of Education and other public and private entities, the International Society for Technology in Education (ISTE) has produced an extensive set of educational technology standards across the curriculum for PK–12 students (Thomas, Bitter, Kelly, and Knezek, 2000). ISTE has also collaborated with the National Council for Accreditation of Teacher Education (1997) to implement technology standards in teacher preparation, urging teacher preparation programs to infuse technology throughout their curricula robustly and energetically. Other major associations have taken similar cooperative initiatives. This book aims to further the cross-disciplinary conversation.

The chapters are organized into two parts, dealing respectively with curriculum and leadership. This is not to suggest a necessary division between these two concerns; they are really two sides of the same coin. We treat curriculum first because we believe that curriculum, above everything else, should drive technology integration. Too often peripheral considerations (the need to appear up-to-date, one-time budgetary windfalls, external grant opportunities, pure politics) have prompted costly technology investments, often without the necessary leadership, professional development, and curricular vision. The disastrous consequences are disheartening because we now know enough about educational leadership to avoid them.

Part One: Curriculum and Pedagogy: The Wellsprings of Leadership

The chapters in Part One deal with issues directly related to classroom implementation. Debbie Abilock examines two classroom projects in research-supported learning and teaching, one focusing on global warming and the other on turn-of-the-century history. In both cases, deep, ongoing collaboration between a library media specialist and classroom teachers spawned curricula that guided student researchers to construct knowledge collectively about the topics under discussion. Abilock highlights the important contribution of global, networked computing to the realization of curricular aims.

Project-centered curriculum of this nature requires careful, theory-based planning. John LeBaron addresses this matter in Chapter Two. He applies Senge's (1990) ideas about learning organizations, weaving discussion about the planning process with commonly accepted principles of curriculum development for technology-rich environments. In the same spirit, in Chapter Three, Eileen Gallagher tackles the challenge of planning for technology in a large, urban district (Chicago). Gallagher depicts systematic links across the urban requirements of funding, infrastructure, professional development, teacher resistance, and community support.

Rounding out the conversation about curriculum, Sanna Järvelä offers practical and theoretical guidance in Chapter Four to readers struggling with the challenge of informing a skeptical public about the pedagogical value of technology investment. Based on naturalistic modes of inquiry, Järvelä offers concrete examples of qualitative research that have generated persuasive evidence about the power of appropriately planned technology applications to promote learning.

Part Two: Leadership Strategies

Recognizing the essential contribution of professional development to technology integration, Catherine Collier launches Part Two. Focusing on the real-life approaches to the curricular integration of technology, Collier probes the theory and practice of professional development, using school-based cases. In Chapter Six, Jyrki Pulkkinen and Merja Ruotsalainen approach Collier's observations from the different perspective of cross-cultural international networks for teacher education. They examine the challenges of Internet-based learning across several countries of the European Union, drawing on the experience of networked teacher training courses that have served adult practitioners from Finland, Italy, the Netherlands, and the United Kingdom.

Effective leadership demands the reconciliation of parochial interests, as diverse stakeholders in and beyond the school building advance their particular agendas in the endeavor to infuse technology. George Perry and Ronald Areglado address the responsibilities of principals as planners, leaders, and managers in Chapter Seven. Applying Kotter's (1996) eight-step process for organizational change, Perry and Areglado urge principals to assume activist curricular roles in promoting the best teaching their faculty can produce, individually and collectively. In Chapter Eight, Isa Zimmerman examines political strategies undertaken in two school systems under her superintendency in a perpetual struggle for change. She describes a systematic strategy for advocacy and change in local, state, and national forums.

Building on Zimmerman's discussion, John Richards reflects in Chapter Nine on the delicate nature of partnerships between schools and the private sector. While endorsing the value of vision-anchored partnerships, Richards suggests that schools need to approach potential collaborators from a strong visionary and moral base, knowing what they want to accomplish, why, and why it is important. The moral question also concerns Linda Friel. Believing in education rather than regulation or sanction as the best foundation for adherence to school policy on appropriate technology use, in Chapter Ten she addresses the roles and responsibilities of teachers, librarians, technologists, and administrators in ensuring ethical, safe student practice. In the context of research and theory, Friel offers practical counsel to educational practitioners in formulating and carrying out policy on intellectual freedom and acceptable technology practice.

Acknowledgments

Assembly of a book such as this takes much effort and patience on the part of authors, editors, and publisher. We are deeply grateful for the time taken not only to develop manuscripts but also for prompt and cheerful responses to what must have seemed like an incessant stream of editorial questions and suggestions. Representing Jossey-Bass, Christie Hakim consistently rendered timely help and wise counsel. We are grateful for the cooperation and good humor so generously offered by everyone associated with this project.

February 2001   John F. LeBaron
                                                   North Chelmsford, Massachusetts
                                                   Catherine Collier
                                                   Shirley, Massachusetts

References

Kotter, J. P. *Leading Change*. Boston: Harvard Business School Press, 1996.

National Council for Accreditation of Teacher Education. *Technology and the New Professional Teacher: Preparing for the 21st Century Classroom*. 1997. [http://www.ncate.org/accred/projects/tech/tech-21.htm].

Senge, P. *The Fifth Discipline: The Art and Practice of the Learning Organization*. New York: Doubleday, 1990.

Thomas, L., Bitter, G., Kelly, M. G., and Knezek, D. *National Educational Technology Standards for Students: Connecting Curriculum and Technology*. Eugene, Ore.: International Society for Technology in Education, 2000.

The International Network
of Principals' Centers

The International Network of Principals' Centers sponsors periodicals and other publications as part of its commitment to strengthening leadership at the individual school level through professional development for leaders. Back issues of *New Directions for School Leadership*, formerly published as a quarterly journal, are now available, and upcoming publications will be available from Jossey-Bass. The network has a membership of principals' centers, academics, and practitioners in the United States and overseas and is open to all groups and institutions committed to the growth of school leaders and the improvement of schools. It currently functions primarily as an information exchange and support system for member centers in their efforts to work directly with school leaders in their communities. The network's office is in the Principals' Center at the Harvard Graduate School of Education.

The network offers the following services:

- The International Directory of Principals' Centers features member centers, listing contact persons, center activities, program references, and evaluation instruments.
- The Annual Conversation takes place every spring; members meet for seminars and workshops, to listen to speakers, and to initiate discussions that will continue throughout the year.
- *Newsnotes*, the network's quarterly newsletter, informs members about programs, conferences, workshops, and special-interest items.

- *Reflections*, the annual journal, includes articles by principals, staff developers, university educators, and principals' center staff members.

For further information, please contact:

International Network of Principals' Centers
Harvard Graduate School of Education
8 Story Street, Lower Level
Cambridge, MA 02138
(617) 495-9812
(617) 495-5900 (Fax)
inpce@gse.harvard.edu

The Editors

John F. LeBaron is professor of education at the University of Massachusetts Lowell. He has authored or coauthored several books, including *A Travel Agent in Cyber School: The Internet and the Library Media Program* (1997, Libraries Unlimited). In 1998–1999, LeBaron undertook a year-long Fulbright scholarship in educational technology at the University of Oulu in Finland. In 2001, he was awarded the Gulbenkian visiting professorship in education at the University of Aveiro in Portugal. His e-mail address is John_Lebaron@uml.edu.

Catherine Collier is a technology specialist with the Shirley, Massachusetts, School District and adjunct professor of technology in education for Lesley University in Cambridge, Massachusetts. She coauthored *A Travel Agent in Cyber School: The Internet and the Library Media Program*. Collier is a member of the Association for the Advancement of Computing in Education, the Association for Supervision and Curriculum Development, and the International Society for Technology in Education. She may be reached at catherine.collier@gte.net.

The Contributors

Debbie Abilock is editor of *Knowledge Quest*, published by the American Association of School Librarians. She also serves as curriculum, library, technology coordinator at the Nueva School, Hillsborough, California. She may be contacted at debbie@nuevaschool.org.

Ronald J. Areglado is principal of the Potowomut School in Warwick, Rhode Island. He is former associate executive director of programs for the National Association of Elementary School Principals. His e-mail address is rid25482@ride.ri.net.

Linda de Lyon Friel is supervisor of media services for the Methuen Public Schools, Methuen, Massachusetts, and coauthor, with John LeBaron and Catherine Collier, of *A Travel Agent in Cyber School: The Internet and the Library Media Program* (1997). She can be reached by e-mail at lafriel@methuen.k12.ma.us.

Eileen M. Gallagher is an administrative technology coordinator for the Department of Learning Technologies, Chicago Public Schools. She also teaches graduate-level classes in instructional technology for Northern Illinois University, DeKalb, Illinois, and for Lesley University, Cambridge, Massachusetts. Her e-mail address is egallagher@kiwi.dep.anl.gov).

Sanna Järvelä is a professor on the Faculty of Education at Finland's University of Oulu, where she directs the Learning and Technology research group. Widely published, she specalizes in qualitative research methodology. She has been honored with a research fellowship award by the Finnish Science Academy and may be reached at sjarvela@ktk.oulu.fi.

George S. Perry Jr. is director of the consulting group Perry and Associates and is senior consultant with the Panasonic Foundation. He may be contacted at perry123@cape.com.

Jyrki Pulkkinen serves as manager of the Educational Technology Research Unit at the University of Oulu in Finland. He has worked as a manager and a researcher in several networked teacher education projects within the European Union and is representing Finland as an educational technology consultant in South Africa. He may be reached at jyrki.pulkkinen@oulu.fi.

John Richards is senior vice president and general manager of Turner Learning, the educational division of Turner Broadcasting System. Turner Learning is responsible for outreach for the networks and for the daily, commercial-free, cable news program *CNN NEWS-ROOM*. Prior to joining Turner, he managed the Educational Technologies Department at Bolt Beranek & Newman in Cambridge, Massachusetts. He has taught at several colleges and universities. His e-mail address is John.Richards@turner.com.

Merja Ruotsalainen is a researcher and teacher in the Educational Technology Research Unit at the University of Oulu. She has designed and taught several internationally networked courses for educators, and specializes in student support systems for on-line learning environments. She may be reached at mruotsal@ktk.oulu.fi.

Isa Kaftal Zimmerman is division director of the Technology in Education Program at Lesley University in Cambridge, Massachusetts. She is the former superintendent of the Acton and the Acton-

Boxborough Regional Public School systems in Massachusetts, as well as a former high school principal and teacher. She actively participates in a variety of educational leadership groups in Massachusetts, throughout the United States, and internationally. Her e-mail address is ikzimmer@mail.lesley.edu.

Technology in Its Place

Part One

Curriculum Integration

Chapter One

Using Technology to Enhance Student Inquiry

Debbie Abilock

Technology plays a vital role in the research
process, but the focus is always on student
thinking. In the examples in this chapter, the
collaboration between librarian and content-area
teachers produces a rich environment for student
investigation.

Fundamental to the collaboration between librarians and other
educators is the design of curriculum for active, authentic student
learning. Wiggins and McTighe (1998) postulate that engaging
students in open-ended, complex, and authentic tasks at the heart
of a discipline is central to deep understanding and the true goal of
education.

The American Association of School Librarians and Association for Educational Communications and Technology (1998)
defines the information-literate student as one who has "the ability to find and use information." Educators are charged with being
"a community of learners . . . centered on the student and sustained
by a creative, energetic library media program" (p. 1).

The American Library Association defines information literacy
as follows: "Information literate people are those who have learned
how to learn. They know how knowledge is organized, how to find
information, and how to use information in such a way that others
can learn from them. They are people prepared for lifelong learning"

(American Library Association, 1999, p. 3). Such students are able to recognize when information is needed and have the ability to locate, evaluate, and use effectively the needed information.

Taxonomies of this research process, such as those developed by Eisenberg and Berkowitz (1990) and Stripling and Pitts (1988), present models of an information problem-solving process requiring common critical thinking attributes across all disciplines. Students generate questions, which focus their definition of their task, look at the sources and assess the quality of the information, examine assumptions and the implication of those assumptions, scrutinize relevant points of view including their own, and come to reasoned judgments. They apply and use standards of reasoning such as clarity, accuracy, relevance, logic, and significance. Finally, through metacognitive awareness, students anticipate and monitor Kuhlthau's stages of feelings (1989) and reflect on the quality of their product and performance. They can then apply their new understandings to their next investigation.

Research Design, Process, and Outcomes

In problem-based learning, students are confronted with ill-structured problems that mirror an authentic situation. It is important for them to recognize that just as in real-world problems, there are no simple right and wrong answers. The challenge for students is to understand complex issues, develop an informed and defensible position, locate data supporting their point of view, recognize information that is relevant, and evaluate the authority of sources. The process of narrowing a topic, creating a hypothesis, and selecting a feasible chunk of a bigger problem is common to all projects in every discipline.

Students must engage in ongoing reflection about the quality and appropriateness of the information they are gathering:

- How much information do I need?
- What did I learn today?

- Am I off-track?
- What am I missing?
- Where should I go next?
- Do I have enough information to draw a conclusion?
- Are all of my conclusions supported by my data?

At Nueva School—a middle school in Hillsborough, California—we (the staff and teachers) believe that throughout the curriculum, students should pose questions, construct meaning, and acquire skills by performing authentic, complex tasks of increasing challenge (Abilock, 1999a).

Collaboration Between
Librarian and Subject Specialists

Creating a research center to support this process is the goal of the school librarian and the subject specialist working collaboratively. Real-world problems often inspire our research projects and generate service learning activity at Nueva, as an example shows.

One hot summer evening in August 1997, while developing an energy curriculum, our science specialist heard President Clinton make a speech on setting national priorities about global warming as a prelude to a conference to be held in December. Nearly 170 countries were to meet in Japan to negotiate an agreement aimed at slowing the buildup of carbon dioxide in order to reduce global warming and its consequences. It was obvious that global warming would be a hot topic that fall, generating substantial debate because of economic interests, scientific differences, and political implications. During late August and early September, we did hours of reading and on-line research to understand the issues better. We searched various information sources to locate materials that students could comprehend and used them to create a Web resource comprising challenging activities and references reflecting the range of controversy that was already permeating the press (Abilock, 1999b).

During what became known as the Global Warming project and while writing narrative evaluations, we spent hours discussing the students, the curriculum, and what could be done differently. Our deliberations were based on observations of students during class and during the final simulation, a review of the research materials students chose to use, examination of students' notes and culminating written work, and input from other teachers. Evaluation of the process and product became a multidimensional learning experience for everyone involved.

This collaborative learning and teaching model occurs frequently at Nueva. The examples that follow demonstrate the integration of information literacy with subject research and the role of technology in constructing deep understanding.

Science Curriculum Example: Global Warming

The science program at Nueva is "hands-on, minds-on, feet-in-the mud," which means that it consists of experiments, simulations, and activities from which students construct an understanding of science concepts. Because it is also important to appreciate the relevance of science to students' lives and to society as a whole, students increasingly spend time extending and generalizing the knowledge gained from experiential learning as they move through the grades. The science specialist's choice of content topics, such as acid rain or plate tectonics, may vary from year to year based on timely events, integration with other disciplines, or even students' interests, but science process skills are a constant. Thus, as curriculum, library, and technology coordinator, I expect to integrate the information literacy skills into a curriculum as it develops over time.

We developed Global Warming as a sixth-grade science-based simulation integrating research, writing, speaking, science lab, and computer skills (see Figure 1.1). The intense controversy among experts about the nature and impact of global warming would allow students to experience thinking within both the science and library disciplines, using the habits of mind (Abilock, 2000a) and creative reasoning that scientists and negotiators would employ during the December 1997 Kyoto Conference. We planned that each student would develop a character representing a particular viewpoint and would participate as that individual in what we referred to as the Nueva Conference on Climate Change (NCCC). The NCCC was a simulation of the Kyoto Conference. Students dressed in character would assemble to debate the critical issues from various points of view and then negotiate solutions to produce a treaty acceptable to all participants. We chose a November date for our conference so we would finish in time to follow the actual events leading up to the Kyoto Conference and allow students time to communicate with their elected representatives. The science specialist was asked to develop a basic background in energy and global warming with

Figure 1.1. Global Warming: Using Technology
for Higher-Order Research, Thinking, and Communication.

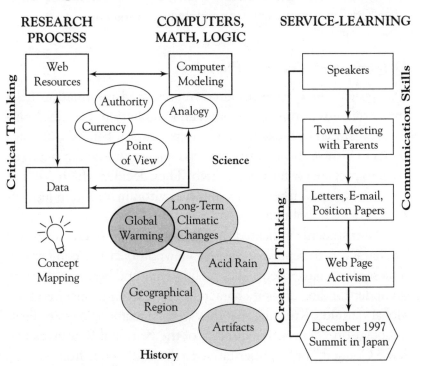

students during science periods extending over fourteen hours. The library research and the simulation (also extending over fourteen hours) would be team-taught.

During science periods, students spent several weeks accumulating basic knowledge through experiments, simulations, and reading. One experiment compared heating of an open container to a closed container. By graphing their data, students observed that the closed container is a more effective heat trap, modeling the greenhouse effect. A more accurate approximation of the actual greenhouse effect was a simulation game that mimicked the absorption of infrared photons by carbon dioxide. In another experiment, students collected gas samples from room air, human breath, car exhaust, and the vinegar-soda reaction and tested them for carbon dioxide concentration to compare the natural sources of carbon dioxide with that from the burning of fossil fuels (Hocking, 1992). To help students appreciate the array of opinions and predicted effects, we began to team-teach reading strategies, using a series of current *New York Times* news articles on global warming.

Defining, Focusing, and Planning

Our project Web page resources represented information from industries, environmental groups, and conflicting scientific opinions, organized by broad interest groups. In October, we asked students to browse through the points of view expressed in our Web page to prepare for further research. They decided which point of view to explore further, for example, environmentalist, industrialist, scientist, or politician.

After students indicated their preferred role, we created a cast of characters to represent various viewpoints at the conference. The students gave themselves pseudonyms and began to develop an understanding of their characters' interests and concerns about global warming. Knowing that they were "director of Western Fuels Association," "executive director of the National Resources Defense Council," or "representative to the conference from Japan," for example, served to sharpen the students' focus and direct their investigations. Questions included, "How will tax credits affect the fossil fuel industry?" and "Does the scientific evidence show sustained trends in climate variability?"

When the science specialist works on a science experiment, such as during the Global Warming project, she coaches all students to visualize the concrete steps that they need to take to answer the questions posed by a hypothesis. Students develop criteria for collecting data to test the hypothesis, devise a procedure to control variables, and develop a materials list and time line. Similarly, as we help students design a research plan, they have to identify likely sources or potential mentors, brainstorm synonyms as keywords, construct Boolean search strings, and create to-do lists and time lines. Typically students are eager to forge ahead with the experimentation or searching, while the teacher or librarian attempts to slow the process to ensure clarity and rigor.

Gathering, Organizing, and Analyzing Data

We grouped students into alliances based on common interests (such as health and environmental interests, corporate groups concerned with profitability, and representatives from low-elevation areas) so they could help one another flesh out their positions. We monitored the social and emotional temperatures of these groups to ensure that they remained productive. The more interested the students became in their roles for the conference, the less intervention and monitoring of the group process was necessary.

Over a three-week period, we met once a week with students for two-hour blocks to examine, select, highlight, and take notes from Web resources, current newspaper clippings, and articles from the library's magazine database.

In a science project, careful observation and accurate recording of the experimental results, followed by analysis and graphing of the data for each variable tested, are essential. In the information literacy model, students select and record data that may be useful, later discarding less relevant information. In both processes, there are several rounds of data gathering as the student develops additional questions, gains expertise, or anticipates opposition arguments or problems.

Drawing Conclusions, Forming Convictions

In scientific research, the conclusions and discussion produce a written synthesis of one's understanding. An original interpretation of evidence should be part of any library information problem solving. Teachers should not mistake a report (the restatement of information) for research (an analysis of information). Furthermore, any culmination or product should display integrity to the process. In the Global Warming project, the product was a simulated conference with persuasive speeches, negotiated solutions, and voting to determine global policy, similar in purpose to the actual event in Kyoto.

At the NCCC event, students dressed in character as delegates and lobbyists assembled before their parents. Student-operated cameras represented the media. Delegates presented their positions in prepared, two-minute, videotaped speeches to the global assembly. Then they broke into working groups composed of two country representatives and a group of lobbyists. These meetings simulated the dilemmas that the real delegates would face as they tried to negotiate the best solution among developing countries, industrial nations, business and environmental interests, and scientists. Each committee's task was to hammer out the specific details of a treaty to be presented back to the assembly by the country representatives. This "thinking on your feet" was the synthesis, an authentic assessment of the depth of each student's understanding. After hearing the proposals from each working committee, the entire assembly of students, parents, and visitors voted to select a global treaty.

In the current climate of strongly held beliefs about global warming, we felt it was necessary for students to voice their personal opinions and examine specific ways in which they could have an impact on this problem. They therefore sent e-mail to congressional representatives, President Clinton, and Vice President Gore. In science class they calculated their own use of energy, used newspaper clippings brought in by students to follow the events, and discussed the political maneuvering leading up to the Kyoto Conference.

Evaluating the Process and the Product

Immediately after the NCCC, students organized their research materials into folders and then composed brief summaries of their characters' positions as part of the Web pages created for the project. This "publishing" for a real audience served to demonstrate how well they could synthesize their understanding. In written self-evaluations, they assessed their research process, as well as their effectiveness in collaborating with their allies, their oral presentations, and their committee work during the simulation. Each student considered the following questions: Why were some sources better than others? How effective were my time line and organization? How well did I think on my feet when challenged? What would I do differently? The last question was a useful way to elicit feedback about how successful they felt and what learning they might transfer to the next project.

Humanities Curriculum Example:
Turn-of-the-Century Child

Students ordinarily believe that history is the recording of facts and that their job is to learn important dates, events, and people. In fact, historical inquiry relies on posing questions about original source documents in order to construct interpretations of history. Historians do research to uncover texts to be analyzed for their assumptions, inferences, and points of view. Thinking like a historian means asking questions—for example:

The question of source: Who created this document (or picture, or relic, or something else)? What was the author's motive? What was the point of view?

The question of context: In what framework was this created? What was the time, and what was the place? In what political climate, social milieu, and cultural context?

The question of credibility: How does this source fit with what I already know and with other evidence I can find from the same period?

On the eve of the new millennium, we created "Turn-of-the-Century Child" to place middle-school students in the role of historians researching the life of a child at the turn of the century 1900 (Abilock, 1999c). Students acted as if they were practicing professionals and incorporated a genuine information problem-solving process (library research) into all aspects of their project. They formulated questions, researched the historical record, and considered multiple perspectives and judgments. Beyond a working knowledge of the events, ideas, and persons of the century, students constructed an understanding of the major themes of the period and how these might affect a child born in 1900. Based on their analyses, they assembled a physical and digital album of letters, oral histories, artifacts, diary entries, narratives, and images based on an invented child within a family. From their investigations students learned to describe the past through the eyes of those who were there and create hypothetical, historically plausible narratives for their individual characters.

Students functioned in two roles. As scholars, they developed historical thinking skills with which they could research and evaluate evidence, interpret the historical record, develop causal analyses, and construct sound historical interpretations. And as unique characters living in different regions of the United States, of different ethnicities, social and economic levels, and genders, they experienced and reflected on the impact of events, ideas, movements, and people on their respective lives.

A series of on-line research investigations supported the students' acquisition of knowledge and helped them locate the visual materials and develop the written texts for their project scrapbooks. Gradually each student developed a character with a personality, feelings, and ideals—a child whose life could be documented in a scrapbook from birth to the moment when the adolescent left home.

"The More You Look, The More You See" was a structured sequence of activities analyzing visual artifacts collected on project Web pages (Abilock, 1999c). The activity was designed to develop reflective capacity, observation, deduction and inferencing skills, clarity and specificity in writing, and the ability to link historical knowledge and particular artifacts. This first series of exercises, using primary source photographs of diverse young children, was designed to teach and practice the skills of observation and deduction to build student understanding of the 1900–1929 era. From digitized photographs taken circa 1900 in different regions of the United States, each student developed a richly realized persona from the same geographic region and ethnic background as the child pictured. Much as a historian fits a particular artifact into an assemblage of evidence to construct a model of the past, students identified, placed, and interpreted these images for their scrapbooks. Each child's scrapbook held photographs, diary entries, letters, oral histories, narratives, and artifacts belonging to an imagined child born in 1900.

A series of Web pages prompted the students to think about events, movements, and themes through the lens of a particular child. For example, "You Are Born in 1900" asked for information about the child's imagined family, in a particular setting, and with a particular heritage. Naming the child was an opportunity for a genealogical investigation and for the student's personal reflection about the significance of names. Other Web pages developed a hometown setting, a school experience (or lack of one), socioeconomic attributes, family traditions, and celebratory occasions.

Parallel exercises prompted students to examine personal photographs in order to reinforce visual literacy skills, experience the process of historical inquiry, and recognize that their own lives are part of the historical record. The goal was a full understanding of how knowledge of the past is constructed from evidence that historians interpret. Students developed visual literacy skills (Abilock, 2000b) to understand artifacts and used the primary record, including digital libraries, to formulate historical questions for further research.

Conclusion

Technology plays a vital role in the research process, though it is subservient to the goals of preparing students to think and observe with the lens of the scientist, the historian, and those in other disciplines. Collaboration between librarians and content-area teachers produces a rich environment for student investigation. With the guidance of the librarian and the subject specialist, students construct their own inquiry by formulating questions and developing hypotheses, preparing time lines and deadlines for their work, and taking a position on a matter that is relevant and interesting to them. Project Web pages and other resources support student research and guide the teacher's and librarian's assessment of the project and the process.

References

Abilock, D. "The Building Blocks of Research." [http://www.nuevaschool.org/~debbie/library/research/il/infolit1.html]. 1999a.

Abilock, D. "Global Warming: Science and Society." [http://www.nuevaschool.org/~debbie/library/cur/sci/gw/globalwarm.html]. 1999b.

Abilock, D. "Turn-of-the-Century Child." [http://www.nuevaschool.org/~debbie/library/cur/20c/turn.html]. 1999c.

Abilock, D. "Habits of Mind." [http://nuevaschool.org/~debbie/hom/habits.html]. 2000a.

Abilock, D. "Habits of Mind: Visual Literacy." [http://nuevaschool.org/~debbie/hom/archive1.html]. 2000b.

American Association of School Librarians and Association for Educational Communications and Technology. *Information Power: Building Partner-*

ships for Learning. Chicago: American Library Association. Washington, D.C.: Association for Educational Communications and Technology, 1998.

American Library Association. *Information Literacy: A Position Paper on Information Problem Solving*. Chicago: American Library Association, 1999. [http://www.ala.org/aasl/positions/ps_infolit.html].

Eisenberg, M. B., and Berkowitz, R. E. *Information Problem-Solving: The Big Six Skills Approach to Library and Information Skills Instruction*. Norwood, N.J.: Ablex, 1990.

Hocking, C. *Global Warming and the Greenhouse Effect*. Berkeley, Calif.: Great Explorations in Math and Science/Lawrence Hall of Science, 1992.

Kuhlthau, C. "Information Search Process: A Summary of Research and Implications for School Library Media Programs." [http://www.ala.org/aasl/SLMR/slmr_resources/select_kuhlthau2.html]. 1989.

Stripling, B. K., and Pitts, J. M. *Brainstorms and Blueprints: Teaching Library Research as a Thinking Process*. Englewood, Colo.: Libraries Unlimited, 1988.

Wiggins, G., and McTighe, J. *Understanding by Design*. Alexandria, Va.: Association for Supervision and Curriculum Development, 1998.

Chapter Two

Curriculum Planning for Technology-Rich Instruction

John F. LeBaron

Educators engaged in infusing curriculum and pedagogy with technology will benefit from familiarity with the current literature on the planning process, leadership, management, public policy, and the essentials of theory-based, philosophy-centered curriculum development.

Vision becomes a living force only when people truly believe they can shape their future.

Peter Senge

Purposeful collective action depends on planning. Planning establishes goals and sets the evaluation criteria by which they are measured. It drives activities, shapes relationships, and provides a scaffold for a shared vision of how curriculum should promote learning. The systematic improvement of learning, teaching, and curriculum depends not only on the presence of an effective plan, but also on the participation of many stakeholders in the design and execution of the plan. In his discussion on learning organizations, Senge (1990) offers the following bedrock conditions that inspire effective planning: systemic thinking, open communication, shared vision, accurate data, and perpetual team learning.

Both strategic and operational planning contribute to the cause of effective technology integration in a school's teaching and learning environment. A strategic plan establishes an overall programmatic tone, painting with broad strokes the program's business and informing stakeholders, including principals, lead teachers, curriculum specialists, and technology coordinators, why they are doing what they do. The operational plan is a more detailed accounting of specific programmatic goals, describing key activities and identifying what will be done by whom. Operational plans produce program output statements that describe what conditions will exist at some determined future time as a result of the implementation of the plan. Moreover, they generate a program budget, which defines how an organization's resources will be allocated for the achievement of the various planning goals.

Educational technologists should think of strategic and operational planning as two sides of a single coin. The strategic plan is revisited and refined, as necessary, on a flexible timetable. Since an up-to-date strategic plan is a prerequisite to the operational plan, both need regular and frequent cross-alignment. The operational plan is developed and implemented over a defined period and moves forward from the measured results of the previous operational plan.

Planning for the integration of the technology into the curriculum is a six-stage, progressively narrowing process (see Figure 2.1). The recommended process, derived from the work of Jensen (1982), combines elements of strategic and operational planning. After launching a planning initiative, the following stages of work can guide subsequent activity:

Create a shared vision that justifies the curriculum (strategic plan).

Assess curriculum needs based on a scan of internal and external conditions (strategic and operational plans).

Describe desired goals, activities, and outputs (operational plan).

**Figure 2.1. The Planning Process for Integrating
Technology into the Curriculum.**

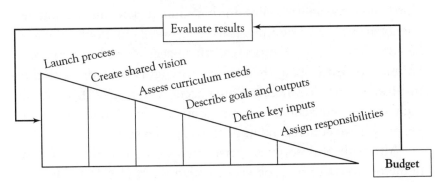

Define key inputs (tasks) required for the desired curriculum
outputs (operational plan).

Assign responsibilities to key management and staff (operational plan).

Evaluate the results of the plan and the process that spawned
it (strategic and operational plans).

Budgeting and planning are closely coupled, but as Figure 2.1
shows, budgeting should be the consequence, not the instigator, of
planning. In other words, planning leads to the budget, though the
budget may lead to an adjustment in plan. Too often educators budget
by making annual adjustments to their existing program lines
and then figuring out what the presumed new budget will buy. But
this practice only reinforces a recycling of time-worn practice and
short-circuits fresh, creative thinking. As the six-stage process is
carried out, attention to Senge's lessons for the learning organization benefits the exercise immeasurably.

Before discussing how planners of technology-rich curriculum
can use this process, it is important to consider a variety of perspectives on curriculum planning.

Planning for the Curriculum

Curriculum specialists maintain that sound curriculum should be anchored by clear commitments to educational philosophy, theory-based visions about learning, realistic images of the learner population, knowledge about their community, and familiarity with the institutional norms where learning occurs (Pratt, 1994). Without such anchors, curriculum remains insufficiently informed. Its components fail to cohere, and its goals risk irrelevance.

Although philosophical perspectives on curriculum are too numerous to count here, observers such as Pratt (1994) and Eisner (1985) identify some important ones:

Essentialism—the belief that curriculum should focus on a limited number of learning essentials and should avoid wasting scarce human and material resources on more marginal matters

Cultural transmission or perennialism—a commitment to transmitting basic tenets of a national or social culture across the generations in order to preserve them more or less in perpetuity

Individual fulfillment—the notion that self-actualization constitutes the most legitimate aims of curriculum, which should be primarily directed toward optimizing the lives of individuals

Social transformation—the belief that curriculum should transform society through advancement of social criticism and political action

Perspectives like this ostensibly kindle curricula designed to serve a greater value, such as the preservation of traditional values, the betterment of society, or the development of happy and secure individuals. Linked closely to such perspectives are theories about how students learn. A behaviorist might suggest that knowledge is external to the individual and that people produce objective evidence of learning by demonstrated behaviors, such as measured performance on tests or precisely defined exercises. Constructivists, on the other hand, believe that knowledge is internal and subjective, shaped by an evolving interaction between unique personal experience and the new phenomena (people, ideas, problems, materials and events) that individuals bring to them. Because no two human experience sets can be identical, constructivists believe that there is no "objective" knowledge.

Since perennialism is committed to the transmission of an externally defined cultural reality, a curriculum based on it might apply techniques derived from the behaviorist, means-ends view of learning espoused by Tyler (1949). Goals and objectives would lend themselves to behavioral descriptions, with curricular content delivered by highly specific activities pursued under precise conditions. Assessment would be keyed to precise measurements of observed student behaviors related to the learning objectives. Such an approach lends itself to a form of technological intervention, manifested in standardized drills and programmed exercises designed for student repetition until all the preset conditions of an objective or goal are mastered. The technology would serve the learners with predetermined menus of "knowledge" and strict rules for accessing and demonstrating it.

The individual fulfillment perspective might find constructivism better suited to its overarching aim. A curriculum dedicated to optimizing human potential will find comfort in a learning theory that stresses individual differences. Curricular goals (predetermined or incidental) might be defined in terms of knowledge-building interactions. Learning environments would be designed for variety and richness, better to optimize the range of interaction available to serve diverse learning styles. Student assessment would emerge from portfolios of work produced either individually or cooperatively. Technologies for this approach would be integrated throughout the learning environment, supporting research and knowledge construction through local databases, worldwide networks, data manipulation software, and multimedia production. Here, students control the technologies that nourish individual learning growth rather than responding to a menu of packaged knowledge items.

Strategies for Planning

Keeping in mind the multiple perspectives on curriculum and learning theory, we review the six stages of curriculum planning and examine how these might inform planners of technology-rich curricula.

Stage 1: Creating the Shared Vision for Curriculum

Planners such as MacDonald (1995) typically reflect Senge's advocacy for stakeholder participation in the planning process. This means that the key people involved in developing technology-rich curricula are given an authentic opportunity to influence the vision and the final shape of the curriculum. This demands a visible process for gathering "vision inputs" and communicating how they will aid in shaping the several curriculum elements. One such visionary input could be that rubric-scaled performance assessment based on computer-generated student portfolio entries will be incorporated into the school curriculum.

School principals are not only key members of guiding coalitions for change; they are also primarily responsible for assembling the team and providing its charge (see Chapter Seven). Other stakeholding members are leading teachers, technology support personnel (coordinators and media librarians), parents and other community members, representatives of the business community (see Chapter Nine), and in some cases students.

Shared values shape curriculum goals and generate individual commitments to meeting those targets. Moreover, coalition members bring perspectives, expertise, and resources to the planning process. With proper team leadership and staff coordination, coalition members can be assigned to subcommittees to pursue specialized planning aspects in the context of the organizational vision, the technology goals, and the overall work of the whole team.

Stage 2: Assessing Curriculum Needs

Based on a realistic scanning of the internal and external pedagogical environments, the accurate assessment of curriculum needs is a critical planning step. When curriculum planners scan, they survey current and anticipated conditions in and outside the school that might influence the nature and execution of the plan. Scanning reflects the systems thinking approach that Senge (1990) advocated. Without it, planning occurs in an informational vacuum, unable to pinpoint constituent characteristics, problem solutions, appropriate resources, or plausible future trends.

Future school scenarios are envisioned in terms of mission and pedagogy. Not only are general descriptions of the student population needed (their demographics, culture, and community attributes, for example), but planners must also consider the broad range of individual learning needs and styles, with a view to applying technology's unique capacities to meet the full scope of learner diversity. Environmental scanning also takes into account current inventories of equipment, space, software, materials, and personnel.

External environmental factors need to be taken into account too. Paramount among these are the emerging state and national frameworks around which curriculum and pedagogy must, for better or worse, be anchored. Such frameworks may or may not be expressed as public mandates, but even when they are not, they typically drive the measurement criteria by which student (and hence, school) performance is evaluated. They cannot be ignored. (A broad-based directory of curriculum standards and education benchmarks is located at the Mid-continent Research for Education and Learning (MCREL) Web site: http://www.mcrel.org/standards-benchmarks/.)

When curriculum planners scan existing conditions, they are performing the "what is" part of a needs assessment. After considering desired futures, resources, and stakeholder interests, they visualize "what should be." The difference between the two equals the program need:

"What Should Be" – "What Is" = Need.

Planners may limit the scope of needs assessment to key people within the program's service population. Alternatively, the community as a whole (including students and parents) can be surveyed. The first approach allows key inside people such as teachers and department heads, who are deeply familiar with the curriculum and the surrounding environment, to contribute in-depth perspectives. The danger, however, is that by themselves, inside personnel may represent vested interests, keen to maintain the status quo and isolated from the concerns of a broader stakeholding population. Assessing the needs of broader populations can strengthen curriculum improvement, especially when such improvement requires external resources and broad-based support.

Needs may be assessed in a variety of ways: written questionnaires, interviews, suggestion boxes, personal observations, and structured information gathering (for example, conducted at academic department or parent-teacher association meetings). Locally networked computer bulletin boards are especially useful instruments for assessing needs. The Internet and district intranets can be used for on-line surveys to gather stakeholder information. After the needs assessment information is gathered and processed, it can help to develop constituent support for curricular change. Such information provides the opportunity to publicize goals and articulate plans for addressing unmet needs.

Stage 3: Describing Desired Goals, Activities, and Outputs

Output statements can be very specific. On one level, they describe specific curricular intentions in precise, behaviorally observable terms—for example, "By the end of this study unit, students will demonstrate no fewer than five types of information sources for

European philosophers who influenced the framers of the Declaration of Independence."

On another level, however, outputs would describe in more general terms the kinds of knowledge production expected as evidence of purposeful interaction with curriculum-centered resources. The character of the output statements would reflect the overall perspective driving the curriculum. Indeed, in constructivist environments, since individual students represent significant variations in input to any learning interaction, they will invariably generate unanticipated differences for each generally articulated output. Recognizing this, some ambiguity should be valued. Output statements of this kind would concern themselves more with the nature and quality of interaction than with the precise behaviors exhibited for evident mastery of predetermined conditions. For this reason, the elements of goal and output setting are combined with activity design in a single curriculum planning strategy.

Schwab (1970) and Eisner (1985) are leading advocates for curriculum aims based on phenomena beyond the strictures of precise objectives. They depict curriculum as art as well as technique, making a case for planners to declare proposed interactions (environments, events, resources, and activities) on which learners develop and shape their ever-emerging knowledge bases. To think of "outputs" in descriptive rather than strict behavioral terms offers rich opportunity to the constructivist-leaning technologist, notwithstanding Apple's (1998) cautions about the technological curricula. With the strategic deployment of computers, applications, and network links, the range and variety of possible interactions between learners and their surrounding environments can be multiplied many times. (Chapter One depicts compelling images of such technology in action.)

Stage 4: Defining Key Curriculum Inputs

Curriculum outputs describe desired conditions, not necessarily behaviors. Inputs describe what it takes to achieve them. Returning to the example about European philosophers who influenced the Declaration of Independence, one of the general outputs was to develop learner research skills by identifying at least five information sources that support this subject.

What key inputs does this output require? Information sources must be available, and the facilities for accessing them are needed. Experienced and trained adults are required not only to find the sources but also to make sense of them and provide a meaningful curricular context. Resources for staff development are required to support the resultant pedagogies and curriculum integration techniques. Information networks of sufficient capacity must be established and maintained. Particular resources will need to be screened, catalogued, and aligned with ongoing curriculum. Appropriate staff development must be organized with sufficient publicity to attract participation. Key input items—technical, material, informational, and human—not only need definition but also a clear strategy for allocation and deployment.

Deployment must be in places where learners work, whether in the classroom, the media center, a computer lab, or some combination of these. (Chapter Three addresses the technological capacities needed for effective deployment in urban settings.) As with all other aspects of the planning strategy, one of the most important planning factors is cohesion among the disparate parts of the technology-rich plan. Inputs must relate to the outputs, which in turn address realistically ascertained needs focused on the fulfillment of a guiding curricular vision.

When all the planning is done, budgetary inputs call for attention. Well-articulated, theory-supported curriculum becomes a powerful tool for properly keyed budget requests. Initial budgets, however, are rarely approved as they stand. Once the budget request is revised, curriculum planners need to adjust. Some elements may need to be dropped, certain goals may need to be scaled back, or other goals may need to be added. Although budgeting is critically connected to curriculum, substantive planning comes first.

Stage 5: Assigning Personal Responsibility

Various school staff members will need appropriate assignments to put elements of the new plan into play. With the enrichment that technology makes possible comes the complexity of skills required to actualize it. Thus, the curriculum planning team depends on the diverse knowledge and experiences that teachers, administrators, technology specialists, librarians, and skilled community representatives can bring to the table.

Senge's call for open communication, data-centered analysis, shared endeavor, and team learning serves this aspect of the planning enterprise most aptly. Those personnel affected by the plan should be consulted so that their concerns may be heard before they are asked to act. This way, leaders can take measures to deal with resource gaps and skill deficiencies. If the implementing stakeholders are not involved in resource identification, then they might well dismiss the value of resources provided externally. Their good ideas for viable alternatives to unaffordable resources would remain untapped. Consultation not only optimizes human capital; it is also good politics. (Chapter Five expands on this point.)

Stage 6: Evaluating and Assessing Results

Curriculum implementation is a continuing process, subject to review, reassessment, and evaluation at any time. Evaluation and assessment occur on two equally important fronts: student learning and the implementation process. A good curriculum plan contains its own summative and formative evaluation components. A summative evaluation is a final accounting of relative success in achieving goals. It is keyed to specific criteria defined in the plan's stated outputs and is reported to program stakeholders, typically at the end of a specified period. A formative evaluation is designed for offering feedback at various stages of implementation and for midcourse improvement as the plan is carried out.

Learner outcomes in technology-enriched curriculum should be measured by assessment tools suitably aligned to transformed practice (see Chapter Four). Thus, visions, needs, goals, and inputs must cohere with the tactics used to measure success. When we think of technology-enriched learning as transformative and "constructive," rather than replicative and "instructive," we think of fundamentally different experiences with different goals and different roles for learner and teacher alike. Performance should therefore be assessed accordingly.

Resources for Technology Planning in the Curriculum

Headquartered at Mississippi State University, the National Center for Technology Planning (NCTP) is a first-rate clearinghouse for information on educational technology planning. In addition to housing exemplary plans, this service offers a variety of Internet-accessible resources germane to planning. The NCTP site (http://www.nctp.com/) includes fertile links to other national, state, and local locations. Of particular interest is its *Guidebook for Developing an Effective Instructional Technology Plan*, developed in 1996 by its director, Larry Anderson, and his former students.

The North Central Regional Educational Laboratory (NCREL; http://www.ncrel.org/tandl/homepg.htm) offers a comprehensive technology planning Web site that provides valuable information on educational perspectives, setting priorities, needs assessment, creating planning committees, and evaluating results. Particularly helpful are the links to pertinent external sites.

Among the best journals for planners are Jamie McKenzie's *From Now On* (http://www.fno.org/index.html). For a curriculum integration emphasis, *Classroom Connect* (http://www.classroom.com/) is helpful. The International Society for Technology in Education journal, *Learning and Leading with Technology*, presents a consistently high standard of discussion for academic and administrative planning alike. (Preview highlights may be found at http://www.iste.org/L&L/index.html.)

Many additional resources for educational technology planning are available on the Internet and in libraries. Planners are urged to read broadly across the educational foundations: curriculum, philosophy, learning psychology, assessment, and program evaluation. Sound educational research, theory, and practice must inform any curriculum planning initiative in order for it to be relevant and effective.

References

Anderson, L., and others. *Guidebook for Developing an Effective Instructional Technology Plan*. Mississippi State University. [http://www2.msstate.edu/~lsa/nctp/Guidebook.pdf]. 1996.

Apple, M. W. "Teaching and Technology: The Hidden Effects of Computers on Teachers and Students." In L. E. Beyer and M. W. Apple (eds.), *The Curriculum: Problems, Politics and Possibilities*. Albany, N.Y.: State University of New York Press, 1998.

Eisner, E. *The Educational Imagination*. New York: Macmillan, 1985.

Jensen, D. R. "Unifying Planning and Management in Public Organizations." *Public Administration Review*, 1982, 42(2), 157–162.

MacDonald, R. M. "Using Internet Resources to Enhance School Media Center Services." *School Library Media Quarterly*, 1995, 23(4) 265–269.

Pratt, D. *Curriculum Planning: A Handbook for Professionals*. Orlando, Fla.: Harcourt Brace, 1994.

Schön, D. "Educating the Reflective Practitioner." Paper presented at the 1987 meeting of the American Educational Research Association, Washington, D.C., 1987. [http://educ.queensu.ca/projects/action_research/schon87.htm].

Schwab, J. J. *The Practical: A Language for Curriculum*. Washington, D.C.: National Education Association, 1970.

Senge, P. *The Fifth Discipline: The Art and Practice of the Learning Organization*. New York: Doubleday, 1990.

Tyler, R. W. *Basic Principles of Curriculum and Instruction*. Chicago: University of Chicago Press, 1949.

Chapter Three

Technology for Urban Schools

Gaps and Challenges

Eileen M. Gallagher

Urban schools face particular challenges in
technology integration, illustrated here by a case
study of one urban district plan.

Technology is expensive. Wiring of older schools, electrical upgrades, high-speed Internet access, and purchasing up-to-date equipment to allow every student access are costly endeavors that do not always show an immediate return in student achievement. The maintenance of equipment and networks is also costly, as few schools have staff knowledgeable enough to carry out these responsibilities. In urban school districts, these costs can be so astronomical that it is small wonder taxpayers are asking how their investment is affecting student achievement.

Since the preparation of students to become productive adults is a major aim of schooling, we look to the work world to see the skills that children need to develop. The basic skills of reading, writing, and computation remain critically important. According to *What Work Requires of Schools: A SCANS Report for America 2000* (U.S. Department of Labor Secretary's Commission on Achieving Necessary Skills, 1993), today's workplace is also seeking employees who can work cooperatively, think imaginatively, and problem-solve creatively. Because of the global explosion of information, employers are looking for people who are technologically literate and able to use the Internet to secure relevant and timely information.

In order to provide students with the appropriate education to develop these skills, teachers must be retrained. The majority of teachers in the classroom today were educated to dispense "knowledge" (the "sage on the stage" style of instructor). Transforming these educators into "guide on the side" facilitators of knowledge construction requires major investments in professional development.

Technology for Essential Skills

To provide the means to develop these essential skills, every school needs a high-speed Internet access through integrated services digital network, cable, and high-bandwidth T1 or T3 telephone-wire connections. Internal school wiring (with either high-quality Category 5 copper wiring or fiber-optic cable) should connect every classroom to the Internet through a building-level local area network (LAN) and a district-level wide area network (WAN). Electrical power to the computers should be available on clean power (circuits that are used only by computers). Classrooms need adequate numbers of Internet-ready, multimedia computers, all with access to the LAN. Once a school has some or all of the wiring and equipment in place, teachers and students must possess the skill and sense of purpose to use it. With the required skills in mind, teachers can rethink the way they teach and the types of learning activities they provide for their students.

Urban school districts have a number of difficulties in meeting the challenge of technology integration. Some of the more obvious reasons are the number of schools, the diversity of populations, and the lack of funding. Sometimes local school control has an impact on technology availability and integration. In many urban schools, the age of the school building is a factor. Many of these facilities, beset by asbestos and other environmental toxins, do not easily accommodate the structural changes needed for cabling and powering modern computers and networking equipment.

Wiring Urban Schools

In a small school district of three to eight schools, it is possible to wire one or two schools a year and see the completion of the entire system in three to five years. And if equipment funding is rotated on a building-by-building basis, individual schools might see new equipment every three to four years. This usually is not the case for urban districts with one hundred or more schools. Even if money is available for wiring a large portion of the district, the number of personnel needed to service only one-third of the schools per year is often unavailable. As projects are slowly rolled out under these conditions, it is difficult to predict completion dates.

The extreme population diversities typical of urban school districts pose an array of problems with which smaller, more affluent districts rarely deal. Poverty and disability align with relatively high levels of linguistic diversity vying for scarce educational resources. Technology must compete with these programs and others, such as preschool education, for the limited funds available for the district budget. All of these programs are important, and many produce more immediate, quantifiable results than technology, so they are more likely to get funded.

Funding for Internet Access

Because the tax base in smaller school districts is relatively homogeneous, taxes and bonding issues are more easily sold to the public. In many urban centers, however, large portions of the population are living on incomes below the poverty level or are on welfare. Although their children are in the school system, the local tax base cannot support the capital and operational costs of good schooling.

The federal government has recently stepped in to help. The educational rate (E-rate) for school-based telecommunications and libraries is designed to help schools build Internet access. The E-rate plan helps all schools prepare their school buildings for Internet access by providing a percentage of the cost of wiring and using telecommunication systems. The higher the percentage is of low-income families with children in the schools, the higher is the percentage that the federal government pays, up to a maximum of 90 percent of the costs.

E-rate funding, however, applies only to telecommunications wiring and services. Schools still need to find funding not only for electrical upgrades, facility repair, and purchase of computer equipment, but also for the curriculum redesign and professional development that make effective technology infusion a reality. Moreover, the E-rate remains politically controversial. E-rate advocates therefore must maintain constant pressure to preserve it.

Two Web sites offer more detailed information about the E-rate: the Web site of the Schools and Libraries Division of the Universal Service Administrative Company (http://www.sl.universal service.org/) and frequently asked questions from Electronic School Online (http://www.electronic-school.com/0997f4.html). Fulton (1999) offers a comprehensive directory of on-line E-rate information for educators.

Integrating Technology in the Classroom

In addition to the wiring and hardware issues, urban schools must address the integration of that technology into the classroom. Students need access to the technology and opportunities to use it as part of their educational process. Class schedules must be redesigned to provide these opportunities, and real-life problem-solving situations need to be incorporated into lessons to provide opportunities for developing the higher-order thinking skills required of an intelligent, employable citizenry.

A major obstacle here is often the classroom teacher and how the school defines a successful teacher. Schools typically follow standardized curricula geared to teach students what they need to score well on standardized tests. As long as these tests remain the primary means of judging a school's effectiveness, teachers will resent time taken from the curriculum to try different strategies. In many urban areas, standardized scores tend to be low, so the pressure to raise test scores is intense. As Thornburg (1991, p. 99) points out, "What gets tested gets taught." Successful technology integration must bring the two learning needs together. Preparing teachers to provide this type of educational experience is a major project in an urban school system with thousands of teachers.

Technology-Literate Teachers

In smaller school districts, prospective teachers go through an intensive interviewing process before they are hired. Their ability to use technology and develop problem-solving lessons can be verified. And once they are hired, new teachers have a trial period until they prove they can meet the district and principal's expectations. In many major urban areas, however, the struggle is to find enough certified teachers to fill all the positions regardless of abilities; very few applicants with state certification are turned away. And in many cases, some of the best and brightest young teachers leave the large urban systems after only one or two years due to the tensions and problems they have to face every day. Consequently, many teachers in these systems are not well versed in the latest teaching methods or the appropriate use of technology. An extensive program in teacher recruitment and professional development is a priority for urban schools.

In many districts, spending money on teachers rather than directly on students is not a priority. Even if the schools are wired and have equipment, the appropriate use of these tools is not evident. Large-scale professional development programs are not in place to change teaching styles. As a result, little change is happening, and justifying the expense of a full-scale technology program becomes harder.

Technology Infusion in the Chicago Public Schools

Chicago has the third largest public school system in the United States, and like many other urban systems, the Chicago public school (CPS) system is devoting a major portion of its budget to developing an infrastructure to support technology. Nearly six hundred schools, spread over 228.5 square miles, serve more than 420,000 students. One of the problems faced by CPS in implementing technology has been the age and condition of many of its school buildings.

Of the approximately 765 buildings, additions, and annexes that make up the CPS, only 14 percent of these are newer than twenty-five years old and have adequate or nearly adequate electrical capacities for technology. Another 26 percent are between twenty-five and fifty years old and are considered upgradable. Over 40 percent of the schools are between fifty and one hundred years old, and these are difficult to upgrade. The worst problems are with the 9 percent of the buildings that are over one hundred years old. (Chicago Public Schools, 1998).

Connecting Students to the Internet

Since 1990 CPS has tried a variety of designs to develop a WAN to connect all buildings and LANs within each building. Every school will have either a T1 line or a T3 line provided by the Chicago Board of Education. These lines will be connected to the CPS center that accesses the Internet through the CPS gateway. Currently almost every school has a T1 line, but most of these lines are not connected to any computers in the school building. The next step is to connect five administrative workstations at each school to the main distribution frame (MDF), where access to the T1 line is available. This phase will connect all of the schools to the WAN for administrative purposes.

Student use of the Internet will depend on the local school's ability to build a LAN connecting classrooms to the MDF. Every school has a discretionary budget based on the number of students, with extra funds for schools with students who are eligible for the federal free lunch program. CPS has a long-range plan to connect ten classrooms and one lab to the network at each school. However, this is at least two to three years away. Therefore, most schools are trying to build their own LANs from discretionary monies.

CPS Funding

The funding of this ambitious project is multifaceted. Special bond issues have provided some of the funds needed to upgrade the schools' electrical and physical structures. The E-rate has been a major influence in making the cost of the wiring and the installation of communication lines attainable. Because of the high percentage of poverty-level families with students in Chicago schools (83 percent), the federal government has picked up 90 percent of the costs for establishing the telecommunications infrastructure. Savings were realized when E-rate funds were made available, and the savings were put back into the project to cover the cost of upgrading the electrical and structural systems in the schools.

LANs are being built through grants, individual school E-rate applications, and the use of a board-funded financial program known as FIN$. This program allows a school to borrow enough money for a major technology project, like building a LAN or upgrading electrical capacity, at a very low rate of interest. The funds can be paid back out of school discretionary funds over three to five years (Chicago Public Schools, 1999).

Planned Use of CPS Communications Infrastructure

Once this entire infrastructure is in place, it will be used for administrative purposes under the auspices of the Department of Informational Technology Services (ITS), and it will service teachers' and students' educational needs through the Department of Learning Technologies (LT).

The ITS Department is responsible for the installation of the WAN connecting all the schools to the central offices for administrative tasks. It also handles all student information, financial data, and personnel information. The LT Department has been charged with the second priority—the task of helping schools integrate technology into their curriculum in the following ways:

- Advising administrators on how to wire their buildings for instruction
- Assisting with developing technology plans, grant proposals, and E-rate applications
- Providing staff development to help teachers and principals learn to use technology appropriately

The LT Department has a field support team known as the Technology Resource Network (TRN) with twenty-eight teachers and one administrator. The TRN services all of the public schools in Chicago. CPS is divided into six regions, each with a technology office in one of its school buildings. Four teachers from the TRN staff each of the six regional offices. The TRN staff members are the primary technology contact people for the approximately one hundred schools in each region. The remaining four TRN teachers work out of the district-wide Medill Professional Development Center. Two of them have primary responsibility for providing technology training for principals. The other two are responsible for all citywide initiatives and maintaining the four LT training labs set up at the Medill Center.

LT Staff Development Activities

One major project of the TRN each year is to organize and provide a citywide technology conference at one of the city's major convention centers. This conference is conducted on a staff development day to allow principals to send teachers without having to provide substitutes. Activities include keynote and spotlight speakers from outside the system, hands-on classes in software applications, between forty-five and seventy-five presentations by CPS teachers and students of technology projects they have completed successfully, and a large vendor fair of the latest technologies. The conference has been an effective tool for increasing interest among the teachers for the integration of technology into the curriculum. The TRN members are then responsible for providing additional professional development at the schools to support this interest and assist teachers in implementing new ideas.

LT also provides the schools with minimum standards for wiring and equipment purchases and approves all purchase orders in these areas to ensure that the standards are met. The newest subdivision of LT is responsible for on-line services. This team designs and maintains the CPS Web page (http://www.cps.k12.il.us/) for the Internet and numerous intranet services for classroom teachers. The main emphasis of this group currently is to help teachers learn how to share lesson plans and ideas on-line and develop on-line classes for their students.

Overall, this massive multidepartmental approach is moving Chicago toward its goal of providing technology access and integration for every student. LT staff are observing that the combined efforts of ITS and LT are having an impact on every school in the district. Judging by the number of teachers enrolling in classes to make use of newly installed Internet access, there is definite progress in the number of schools and teachers using the Internet and moving toward developing active student learners who use technology regularly.

Another Urban School District Model

Other urban school districts face problems similar to Chicago's. Across the nation there is a reform movement to return control of urban schools to the local school population. Although this approach offers benefits, it also creates a challenge to massive technological transformation. Local school control provides little or no central guidance or management. Schools have no central resource for advice on curriculum, wiring, electrical upgrades, or facility renovation. There is no central WAN for professional dialogue.

In Cleveland, most of the funding is spent on purchasing computers and providing staff development. Cleveland used its funds from Ohio's SchoolNet Plus program to provide sixty hours of training to every teacher in grades K–4 and to provide computers in every K–4 classroom. However, these computers are not networked, and few have Internet access. Like Chicago, Cleveland's schools are aging, and the facilities need repairs and electrical upgrades before they can handle a LAN or WAN.

Of the 3,369 classrooms in Cleveland, only about 300 have Internet access, most through dial-up modems. The number of computers available beyond the fourth grade is very small. The ratio of students to computers in the high school classrooms is 209 to 1, and in high school labs it is 47 to 1. The Cleveland School District has applied for E-rate funds to help in wiring schools, but like Chicago, it will need much more for the infrastructure changes needed in most schools (Sweeney, 1999).

Conclusion

National surveys show that the schools least likely to have classrooms connected to the Internet are urban schools. These districts are described as having one thousand or more classrooms with 50 percent or higher minority enrollment and 71 percent or higher of students eligible for free or reduced-price school lunches (National Center for Education Statistics, 1999). The national average of students per computer with Internet access is approximately 20 to 1. Many states with major urban areas fall far below this average; among them are Texas, Florida, California, New York, New Jersey, Pennsylvania, and, lowest of all, the District of Columbia, at almost 67 to 1 (Harrington-Lueker, 1999).

We need to find a way to provide technology to these urban schools where a large percentage of the nation's children are taught.

Preparing all children for viable futures may seem expensive, but it will be money well spent. The cost of graduating class after class of students unprepared to meet the needs of today's and tomorrow's workforce will be far more expensive.

References

Chicago Public Schools. *CPS Technology Plan 1998–2004*. Chicago: Chicago Public Schools, 1998.

Chicago Public Schools. *FIN$ Application Packet*. Chicago: Chicago Public Schools, 1999.

Fulton, D. "E-rate: A Resource Guide for Educators." *ERIC Digests*. [http://www.ed.gov/databases/ERIC_Digests/ed420307.html]. 1999.

Harrington-Lueker, D. "Overview: Making Technology Work in Urban Schools." In P. Pardini and D. Harrington-Lueker (eds.), *Barriers and Breakthroughs: Technology in Urban Schools*. Washington, D.C.: Education Writers Association, 1999.

National Center for Education Statistics. *Advanced Telecommunications in U.S. Public Elementary and Secondary Schools*. Washington, D.C.: National Center for Education Statistics, 1999. (ED 426 694)

Sweeney, S. "Cleveland: Teaching the Teachers." In P. Pardini and D. Harrington-Leuker (eds.), *Barriers and Breakthroughs: Technology in Urban Schools*. Washington, D.C.: Education Writers Association, 1999.

Thornburg, D. *Education, Technology and Paradigms of Change for the 21st Century*. Monterey, Calif.: Starsong Publications, 1991.

U.S. Department of Labor Secretary's Commission on Achieving Necessary Skills. *What Work Requires of Schools: A SCANS Report for America 2000*. Washington, D.C.: Diane Publishing Co., 1993.

Chapter Four

Technology and Learning

Getting the Story Out

Sanna Järvelä

Advocates of technology can publicize the
potential and the successes of technology-based
learning environments to motivate students in a
number of ways, thus promoting improved learning
in restructured schools.

Preparing children for a rapidly changing world is an exacting challenge. Students who enter the information-centered world of this century must be prepared to learn on their own. Learning skills and motivation for lifelong growth are crucial for coping with the continuous challenge of information flow. Technology can play an important role in restructuring teaching and learning practices to match the needs of an information society better. There are many ways in which technology can promote improved learning in restructured schools, and these descriptions offer persuasive strategies for advocates to publicize the success of technology to a skeptical public.

Learning for Understanding Demands More Than Memorization

Given today's information explosion, it is not sufficient merely to memorize a body of knowledge. Internet connections, for example, provide continuous access to rich webs of information. However, learning for understanding does not result simply from access to knowledge, but presumes a learner's lifetime involvement in constructing knowledge both individually and collaboratively (Steffe and Gale, 1995). Citizens educated for an information society are able to reason with and about that knowledge. They make decisions about what they know and what they need to learn. As distinct from knowing facts, understanding information requires the ability to ask questions about interesting, important, and authentic phenomena; formulate hypotheses and theories to answer these questions; collect evidence; and argue and distribute the evidence to others.

According to many learning researchers, traditional instructional approaches based on factual memorization should be replaced with inquiry methods. Inquiry provides opportunities for students to generate their own goals and plan and carry out research to achieve them (Barron and others, 1998; Brown and Campione, 1996). Technology can play an important role in restructuring teaching-learning processes to create highly effective strategies for student inquiry. Knowledge and understanding are constructed not only by individuals, but socially in interaction with other individuals, contexts, and society. Support for shared understanding, negotiation, and social interaction is needed (Scardamalia, Bereiter, and Lamon, 1994).

How Do Technology-Based Models Motivate Students to Learn for Understanding?

By themselves, even the most sophisticated technologies cannot improve learning or thinking. Rather, educators, aided by technology, can create learning environments that support higher-order thinking and constructive discussion. Several recent studies support the hypotheses that learner-centered technologies facilitate task-related motivation and provide social support for students (Bonk and King, 1998; Järvelä, 1998; Järvelä, Niemivirta, and Hakkarainen, 2000; O'Malley, 1995; Scardamalia and Bereiter, 1996). When students are able to work on interesting and challenging tasks, they partici-pate in creating their own learning goals. The learning process thus becomes personally meaningful to them. The higher levels of moti-vation that result promote progressive advances in cognitive en-gagement and application of learning to real-life problems.

Contextual Classroom Principles to Enhance Motivation

Motivation research has demonstrated common principles show-ing how certain dimensions in classroom learning environments can be structured to promote the achievement of learning goals (Ames, 1992; Blumenfeld and others, 1991):

- The task dimension concerns the design of strategies that make learning interesting by ensuring varied activity and personal challenge for learners. This dimension also includes helping students to establish realistic goals.
- The authority dimension stresses students' opportunities to take leadership roles and develop a sense of personal control and ownership in the learning process.
- Evaluation and recognition address the formal and informal use of rewards, incentives, and praise in the classroom. This dimension includes guidelines, such as recognizing individual student effort, accomplishment, and improvement and ensuring that all students receive appropriate rewards and recognition for their achievements.
- The grouping dimension focuses on students' ability to work effectively with others on school tasks. This dimension includes opportunities for social interaction, peer collabora-tion, and varied group arrangements.

Technology-based learning environments can help optimize the achievement of these research-based principles for enhancing student motivation in the classroom. The coupling of wise peda-gogical choices with technology offers a potential for reorganizing the dynamics of student and teacher actions in terms of interactive processes, strategic practice, situational interpretations, and school-community partnerships (Brown and Campione, 1996; Koschmann, 1994).

Organizing Learning Around Interdisciplinary Themes

The organization of learning around broad interdisciplinary big themes has been shown to be an effective and challenging teaching strategy. Technology has been used effectively as a cognitive tool to support the selection and organization of resources in handling complex information, the creation of new knowledge, and the social sharing of the results of intellectual explorations.

From a motivational perspective, thematically structured classrooms support the clarification and pursuit of learning goals (Ames, 1992; Blumenfeld and others, 1991). In such an environment, teachers emphasize the qualitative phases of the learning process in reiterative, formative progress toward conceptual goals. Assessment of these processes takes on greater importance than the development of concrete products and summative evaluations of final performance.

Real-world experiences linked to curriculum both promote motivation and support strategies for continued learning. For example, inquiry learning (Hakkarainen, Lipponen, and Järvelä, forthcoming) offers several advantages for heightening student motivation. Authentic problem contexts provide meaningful cognitive relationships between students and their learning tasks. The process of authentic inquiry starts from epistemological goals that arise from personal cognitive needs that cannot be met by relying on only external knowledge. An essential aspect of knowledge-seeking inquiry is the generation of a learner's own explanations, hypotheses, or conjectures (Brown and Campione 1996; Perkins, Crismond, Simmons, and Under, 1995; Scardamalia and Bereiter, 1992). Participation in such a process fosters a dynamic change of conceptions. It produces learning that is connected to the learner's existing knowledge, providing a rich web of connections and meaning and thereby eliciting effective and purposeful problem solving.

The Social Construction of Knowledge

Technology-supported learning environments contribute to student motivation through their potential for social interaction. In communities of learners, information and expertise may be distributed across individuals and synthesized in collective knowledge construction (Salomon, 1993). For example, peers provide models of expertise that others can observe. Observing the progress of classmates may increase students' confidence in their own ability to succeed (Schunk, 1991). In addition, peer models provide benchmarks for students' own self-evaluations, helping them to set proximal goals for themselves. As research in cooperative learning has shown, working with others promotes students' engagement in their own work (Slavin, 1996). Collaborative learning facilitated by networked technology environments tends to make practices of knowledge processing more accessible and widespread than would be present in conventional learning environments.

Computer Supported Intentional Learning Environment: A Technology Tool for Authentic, Thematic Study

In "big-theme" classroom settings, technology-enhanced environments can facilitate student interaction with authentic problems in unique ways. (A big-theme classroom is one in which student inquiry focuses broadly on essential disciplinary themes.) Students then define their specific research questions in the context of these larger themes. The Computer Supported Intentional Learning Environment (CSILE), described by Scardamalia and Bereiter (1996), is a computer-networked technology that brings the principles of knowledge building and sharing into the authentic practice of learning. Under skilled teacher guidance, CSILE supports student learning by providing tools for inquiry-based activities, discussion, and knowledge production. CSILE is an empty hypermedia database where students create the content. They present their own research questions, intuitive working theories, and new knowledge in the form of textual and graphical contributions.

The basic assumption behind CSILE is that all communication is open to the other members of the knowledge-building community, although individuals may also produce private notes. Such knowledge sharing provides opportunities for all pupils to participate equally in the discourse of a project. CSILE contains tools for producing, storing, seeking, classifying, and linking knowledge by text and graphic processing and discussion utilities. It supports students cognitively by helping them to articulate, explore, communicate, and structure their own knowledge.

Research on Two Technology-Enhanced Projects on Racism

In a research project initiated by Järvelä and Salovaara (1999), a seventh-grade public school class in Oulu, Finland, used CSILE to study the theme of racism. Because the project was carried out in a literacy class, the focus was on developing students' skills in analytical reading and writing. The theme was studied through such diverse instructional activities as interviews, brainstorming, textual analysis of a novel, and student-written dialogues and short stories. The project theme supported some of the main topics in the ongoing school literacy curriculum and also included some unique topical and authentic questions.

The students created subprojects focusing on the theme of racism. The project lasted for six weeks, during which the students engaged in project lessons three times a week. Student understanding of racism was progressively constructed by ongoing collaborative discourse and knowledge distribution in the CSILE environment. The project produced increased student research skills. For example, working with CSILE supported the students' processes of inquiry. Various cognitive tools embedded in the networked environment helped them to structure and implement research-like activities and to participate in collaborative knowledge building (Hakkarainen, Lipponen, and Järvelä, forthcoming; Järvelä, Bonk, Lehtinen, and Lehti, 1999).

To begin their project work, the pupils were introduced to the theme by reading a novel dealing with racism. The themes and the events of the novel were discussed inside CSILE using networked computers. Student discourse was gradually guided from concrete discussion about the content of the book to more general issues around the topic of racism. Next, the students generated their own research questions, which they communicated to the learning group using CSILE. Students posed such questions as, "Are all people racists?" and "When did racism arise?"

The students developed answers to their questions by using a variety of instructional activities and communications tools. For example, they conducted interviews and read resource materials from magazines, books, and the Internet. To help them move from research to active knowledge construction, they then chose their own research topics and planned their investigations. Students conducted deeper analyses of the theme through the critical examination of the novel's text, brainstorming, and writing their own short stories.

The student research procedures and results were documented, stored, and shared in the CSILE database. Students commented on each other's notes and thereby developed their own personal understanding about the theme. Using the CSILE database, all students were able to synthesize the contributions of their peers and summarize their personal perceptions in original essays about the investigation and its results.

Evidence of Constructive Social Interaction

Student learning was assessed through qualitative procedures that produced narrative accounts of project results. Recent studies (Hakkarainen, Lipponen and Järvelä, forthcoming; Järvelä and others, 1999) have reported that a CSILE-based work process can create situations that challenge students to regulate their learning. This is seen in the following student interpretations of working with CSILE in the racism project (the interpretations are excerpts of an interview situation conducted immediately after one of the project lessons):

> "When I wrote my note in the CSILE environment, I was waiting for other students' comments on my note."
> "When I see the other students' notes, I can compare my own ideas to them."
> "I can see how the other students think."

Reinforcing interviews that the researchers conducted with the students show that working with CSILE promoted student communication and comprehension—for example:

> *Interviewer:* What was the meaning of CSILE during the lesson?
> *Student:* I reported about myself and how I had progressed.
> *Interviewer:* Was it useful?
> *Student:* Well, it made me think different things . . . like what to do next.
> *Interviewer:* What was the most interesting thing about CSILE?
> *Student:* I was able to revise my work, I mean to see what I did during the lesson, and then to see what the other students did.

It seems clear that the CSILE learning environment provided a forum for each student's ideas to be shared and processed with the teacher and other students.

Evidence of Student Responsibility and Interest

Effective learning environments support student responsibility for their own learning. The term *autonomy-support* refers to enabling students to make choices, participate in pedagogical decisions, and personally own their learning goals. Higher-level practices of inquiry require a shift in the cognitive division of labor between the teacher and the student and a primary focus on problems rather than roles. Traditionally the teacher unilaterally manages most of the higher cognitive functions in school, such as planning, questioning, explaining, and evaluating, while the students are expected to recall and reproduce the transmitted information.

Scardamalia and Bereiter (1996), however, have argued that an important prerequisite for the development of higher-level cognitive competencies is that students themselves take the responsibility for cognitive (for example, questioning and explaining) and metacognitive (for example, goal setting, monitoring, and evaluating) aspects of inquiry. The transfer of responsibility from the teacher to the student increases student autonomy and control. When classroom environments support student autonomy, students perceive the material as more intrinsically motivating (Grolnick and Ryan, 1987; Turner, 1995).

In another project on a student-centered problem-solving task in a Lego/Logo computer environment, Järvelä's (1995) research demonstrates how a problem context creates a task-oriented teacher-student partnership. (For a detailed account of the Lego/Logo computer environment, see Chapter Six.) With technology, it is possible to create simulated problem situations and external representations of the thinking processes. The context provides conditions for new kinds of teacher-student interaction—interactive conditions in which partners are no longer continuously aware of their roles as teacher and students. Instead, they enter mutually interesting tasks and experiences.

The next episode describes a scaffolding dialogue between the teacher and a student. In this environment, scaffolding discussions (Collins, Brown, and Newman, 1989) with the teacher became more like joint goal-oriented problem-solving collaborations in which the partners pursued an authentic interest in solving a complex problem. In the following example, two student peers are working with their teacher in a Lego/Logo environment designed to program a model for an automated washing machine:

Teacher [to students who are intensely following the explanation]: The problem is that when it stops here, it'll . . . um . . . return to the previous procedure, which then calls . . .

Student 1: Why's that?

Student 2: Yeah. How can you make it stop?

Teacher: Well, the problem's here, you see . . . I don't know how to solve this.

Student 2: I was just thinking that if you put the end in parenthesis and then "end" and "onfor 40" . . .

Teacher: Um.

Student 2: No, no, I mean "to end" and "onfor 40."

Student 1: What? It's going to end at four seconds.

Student 2: [Laughs] . . . and it'll go nuts! Right! So, I just put here "end" and then "talkto a," let's say "onfor 40." [Types it into the computer.]

Student 1: Then the motor should rotate for four seconds.

Student 2: That's right. Will it restart after that?

Teacher: Well, there may be a couple of problems left. [They all try the program out.]

In this episode the teacher and the students are solving a problem together. The teacher indicates that the problem is difficult to solve, but still they are highly involved in solving it, even though it is the end of a lesson. All the partners in this learning episode appear to be equally contributing to a jointly held goal, and nobody wishes to break away from this task.

Translating Research into Public Support

Several studies to date have indicated quite persuasively that carefully designed technology environments hold much potential for student learning (Järvelä, Niemivirta, and Hakkarainen, 2000). What kind of guidance and support, however, do students and teachers need to optimize public investment in technology-supported school improvement? In sophisticated pedagogical practice, technology becomes an integrated part of the whole learning environment. It becomes embedded in the culture of learning. As such, it is used for creating social structures that encourage learning, supporting reflective discourse, and encouraging students and teachers to build communities of learning within and across the disciplinary domains.

Within schools, decisions about which kind of technological infrastructure and models should be acquired need the backing of research- and theory-based argumentation. What kinds of learning processes do alternative theory-based technology environments support? How does the learning environment promote students' task involvement and motivation? Does technology support students' self-regulated learning? Does it support student choice in the selection of learning goals? Does the technology environment provide only access to knowledge, or does it offer tools to discover and work with information?

The literature on educational technology efficacy offers many examples of "objective" research that attempt to reveal the relative merits of technological versus nontechnological practice (Leung and Chung, 1997; Kinnaman, 1990). From the viewpoint of the school-based technology advocate, this kind of positivistic analysis poses two significant problems. First, the research itself is often shallow, pursued in unrealistic "laboratory" settings in an attempt to weigh phenomena that are too complex to warrant direct statistical comparison. Often such research fails to elucidate the singular learning benefits of new practices that are genuinely transformed by technology. Second, when educators rely on such comparisons to make their public case, they engage in a counterproductive discourse that removes them from the rich contributions that they, as experienced teachers, know technology has made possible.

MacColl and White (1998) affirm that "parents, educators, school board members, and legislators all want to know 'what works' 'what does [not]' in terms of educational programs and innovations." Since these lay constituencies control the conduits for all streams of educational investment, they need to know results in terms that both they and those reporting clearly understand.

If we take the research reported in this chapter, for example, results presented to lay audiences would be presented in short, illustrated narratives containing the following information:

- The particular goals of the activity
- The theories and philosophies underlying these goals and activities
- The relationship of goals to the overall school curriculum and mission
- The relationship to broad standards, guidelines, and policies
- Illustrations of the activity in practice
- Examples of student work authentically produced, individually and collaboratively
- Demonstrations of the unique contributions to learning by the technologies employed
- Description of the methods used to assess the results

The message can be communicated effectively by experience-based narratives that indicate what happened, why it is important, how it relates to other important goals, what the students did, and how the researcher knows whether it worked. Most important, such reports highlight the role of technology in a way that makes clear that the achievements reported would not have been possible without it. The results are narrated in terms of the project's intentions, not in terms of general norms that may be only remotely related to these intentions.

Conclusion

Why should the public invest its scarce resources in technology for education? Perhaps a more relevant question would be to ask how we can support the development of students' knowledge and skill to cope in a changing society. One of the basic requirements in educating for the future is to prepare learners for participation in an information and communication society in which knowledge will be the most critical capital asset for social and economic development.

The skills of independent searching, elaborating, managing, and extending knowledge will be critically important in the networked information society of the future. Equally important will be the skill of regulating one's own cognitive activity and productively collaborating with others. Even now, schools are being driven to find better pedagogical methods to cope with these new challenges. Modern technology can play an important role as a tool for restructuring teaching-learning processes to prepare learners better for future, higher-order challenges. Securing the resources to capitalize on technology's potential will require "telling the story" persuasively, in richly descriptive language that constituencies will understand and in terms that educators truly intend.

References

Ames, C. "Classrooms: Goals, Structures, and Motivation." *Journal of Educational Psychology*, 1992, 84, 261–271.

Barron, B., Schwartz, D. L., Vye, N. J., Moore, A., Petrosino, T., Zech, L., and Brandsford, J. D. "Doing with Understanding: Lessons from Research on Problem and Project-Based Learning." *Journal of the Learning Sciences*, 1998, 7, 271–311.

Blumenfeld, P. C., and others. "Motivating Project-Based Learning: Sustaining the Doing, Supporting the Learning." *Educational Psychologist*, 1991, 26, 369–398.

Bonk, C. J., and King, K. S. (eds.). *Electronic Collaborators: Learner-Centered Technologies for Literacy, Apprenticeship, and Discourse*. Hillside, N.J.: Erlbaum, 1998.

Brown, A. L., and Campione, J. C. "Psychological Theory and the Design of Innovative Learning Environments: On Procedures, Principles, and Systems." In L. Schauble and R. Glaser (eds.), *Innovations in Learning: New Environments for Education*. Hillside, N.J.: Erlbaum, 1996.

Collins, A., Brown, J. S., and Newman, S. "Cognitive Apprenticeship: Teaching the Craft of Reading, Writing and Mathematics." In L. Resnick (ed.), *Knowing, Learning and Instruction: Essays in Honor of Robert Glaser*. Hillsdale, N.J.: Erlbaum, 1989.

Grolnik, W. S., and Ryan, R. M. "Autonomy Support in Education: Creating the Facilitating Environment." In N. Hastings and J. Schwiesco (eds.),

New Dimensions in Educational Psychology: Behaviour and Motivation. Bristol, Pa.: Falmer Press, 1987.

Hakkarainen, K., Lipponen, L., and Järvelä, S. "Epistemology of Inquiry and Computer-Supported Collaborative Learning: A Cross-Cultural Comparison." In T. Koschmann, N. Miyake, and R. Hall (eds.), *CSCL2: Carrying Forward the Conversation.* Mahwah, N.J.: Erlbaum, forthcoming.

Järvelä, S. "The Cognitive Apprenticeship Model in a Technologically Rich Learning Environment: Interpreting the Learning Interaction." *Learning and Instruction,* 1995, *5,* 237–259.

Järvelä, S. "Socioemotional Aspects of Students' Learning in Cognitive-Apprenticeship Environment." *Instructional Science,* 1998, *26,* 439–471.

Järvelä, S., Bonk, C. J., Lehtinen, E., and Lehti, S. "A Theoretical Analysis of Social Interactions in Computer-Based Learning Environments: Evidence for Reciprocal Understandings." *Journal of Educational Computing Research,* 1999, *54*(3), 6–10.

Järvelä, S., Niemivirta, M., and Hakkarainen, K. "The Interaction of Students' Self-Reported Motivation and Strategies and Situational Motivation and Action During a Computer Supported Collaborative Learning Project." Unpublished manuscript, 2000.

Järvelä, S., and Salovaara, H. "Computer Supported Collaborative Learning in a Secondary Literacy Classroom—A Quality of Students' Motivational Processes." Unpublished manuscript, 1999.

Kinnaman, D. E. "What's the Research Telling Us?" *Classroom Computer Learning,* 1990, *10*(6), 31–35, 38–39.

Koschmann, T. D. "Toward a Theory of Computer Support for Collaborative Learning." *Journal of the Learning Sciences,* 1994, *3,* 219–225.

Leung, C., and Chung, C. "Student Achievement in an Educational Technology Course as Enhanced by Cooperative Learning." *Journal of Science Education and Technology,* 1997, *6*(4), 337–343.

MacColl, G., and White, K. "Communicating Educational Research Data to General, Nonresearcher Audiences." ERIC Digest ED422406 98. Washington, D.C.: ERIC Clearinghouse on Assessment and Evaluation, 1998. [http://www.ed.gov/databases/ERIC_Digests/ed422406.html].

O'Malley, C. *Computer-Supported Collaborative Learning.* New York: Springer-Verlag, 1995.

Perkins, D. A., Crismond, D., Simmons, R., and Under, C. "Inside Understanding." In D. N. Perkins, J. L. Schwartz, M. M. West, and M. S. Wiske (eds.), *Software Goes to School.* New York: Oxford University Press, 1995.

Salomon, G. *Distributed Cognitions.* Cambridge: Cambridge University Press, 1993.

Scardamalia, M., and Bereiter, C. "Text-Based and Knowledge-Based Questioning by Children." *Cognition and Instruction,* 1992, *9,* 177–199.

Scardamalia, M., and Bereiter, C. "Engaging Students in a Knowledge Society." *Educational Leadership*, 1996, *54*(3), 6–10.

Scardamalia, M., Bereiter, C., and Lamon, M. "The CSILE Project: Trying to Bring the Classroom into World 3." In K. McGilly (ed.), *Classroom Lessons: Integrating Cognitive Theory and Classroom Practice*. Cambridge, Mass.: MIT Press, 1994.

Schunk, D. H. "Self-Efficacy and Academic Motivation." *Educational Psychologist*, 1991, *26*, 207–231.

Slavin, R. E. "Cooperative Learning in Middle and Secondary Schools." *The Clearing House*, 1996, *69*(4), 200–204.

Steffe, L. O., and Gale, J. *Constructionism in Education*. Hillsdale, N.J.: Erlbaum, 1995.

Turner, J. C. "The Influence of Classroom Context on Young Children's Motivation for Literacy." *Reading Research Quarterly*, 1995, *30*, 410–441.

Part Two

Leadership Strategies

Chapter Five

Staff Development for Technology Integration in the Classroom

Catherine Collier

> Four approaches to professional development for
> technology integration illustrate staff development
> plans that leverage local expertise and aim for
> schoolwide improvement.

Preparing and empowering teachers to integrate technology in the classroom is an ongoing process. *Teachers and Technology: Making the Connection* (Office of Technology Assessment, 1995) made the point that the approach many schools took a decade ago did not work. It was not enough to hold workshops or give classes designed to instill computer literacy and hope teachers would apply their new skills in the classroom. Teachers, even those who are computer literate, need a vision of technology in the learning process, and that vision needs to expand as learning technology changes. They need hands-on experience with technology and the challenge and accountability to apply new techniques to curriculum and instruction. They need support to assess and refine their new instructional approaches.

This chapter examines a variety of approaches to staff development for technology. It considers the role of technology directors or consultants, teacher leaders (Katzenmeyer and Moller, 1996), administrators, and students in the ongoing effort. The term *technology specialist* is used throughout to indicate a district-wide director or outside consultant with an advanced degree in education and expertise in educational technology and curriculum, who is familiar with the demands of teaching and has the ability to interact with the central office and secure grants. (For a broad introduction, see Grant, 1996.)

Just as the manner of technology integration should fit the goals of the learning organization (Guskey, 1998), so should the manner of staff development for technology integration (Bray, 1999). It should aim to develop local capacity for ongoing support, leveraging the strengths of the school's curriculum and its teachers. It should employ technology specialists who can extend the vision of the organization, tie in leading-edge resources, and secure funding for new efforts.

In general, preparing teachers to integrate technology in the classroom employs many learning experiences and resources, especially the following:

- Hands-on exercises, focused on the curriculum, with tools such as an office package, multimedia, and Internet browser and e-mail
- Interaction with software packages and a forum to consider their use in the curriculum
- Examples of well-designed lessons, units, and projects that use technology in an integrated fashion
- Instruction in finding and evaluating resources
- Instruction in techniques and technologies for student inquiry, such as probeware, WebQuests, simulations, modeling tools, and design tools
- Instruction in the creation of new resources, such as those produced with video, hypermedia, and authorware

Like all other staff development, success depends on giving teachers time to practice, communicate, and reflect; fostering new vocabulary and habits; and setting expectations and accountability. Little (1982) characterizes effective staff development as "an organizational phenomenon. . . . Some schools sustain shared expectations (norms) both for extensive collegial work and for analysis and evaluation of an experimentation with their practices; continuous improvement is a shared undertaking in these schools, and these schools are the most adaptable and successful" (p. 339).

Approaches to Technology Integration

Four approaches to professional development for technology integration illustrate staff development plans that leverage local expertise and aim for schoolwide improvement. Each empowers and supports teachers, regardless of their technical skill level; each is consistent with the organization and mission of the school; and each focuses on the integration of technology in the curriculum.

Technology Mentors

Mentoring is an honored tradition for preparing new teachers and novices in a field. Mentors guide their protégés by passing along best practices and tricks of the trade, fostering habits of work and habits of mind, and posing challenges to achieve and then exceed high standards. In a school system, technology mentors may be master teachers, or they may be new teachers who bring technology expertise into their new role and are eager to share these skills with veterans who for their part guide their classroom practice and their growing sense of curriculum. Technology mentors are a valuable resource in planning staff development for technology integration. Two examples, from Breithaupt (1998) and Sherwood (1999), illustrate the wide range of possibilities.

Breithaupt recounts a project in which several North Carolina schools, acting as professional development schools in partnership with a large teacher preparation institution, participated in an extensive effort to prepare student teachers to use technology in the classroom and to encourage mentor classroom teachers to integrate technology in the curriculum. The teacher preparation program used its pairing of preservice teachers and in-service teachers to explore educational technology and define its use in the curriculum. The preservice teachers brought to the partnership a large body of technical skills and awareness of new teaching methods, while the in-service teachers contributed years of experience with curriculum development and classroom teaching. Both were interested in using technology as a tool for teaching and learning, with the focus on student achievement.

The school-university partnership provided a strong support mechanism for the effort. A resource team at the university, consisting of faculty, staff, and graduate students, provided technology skills, knowledge of methods and materials, and grant-writing skills. This team supported all the partner schools, sometimes making site visits to educate teachers and library media specialists, and preparing grant proposals in support of curriculum innovation with technology. The partnership was highly beneficial for both sides.

The technology mentor need not be a preservice or a new teacher. Many schools have experienced teachers who are capable of technology integration or have "technology teachers" who are certified classroom teachers specializing in technology integration. Sherwood (1999) describes the pivotal role one such technology teacher played in transforming the Appleby Elementary School in Marathon, New York, into a technology-infused learning organization over a three-year period. In an effort to increase the use of technology in the curriculum, administrators at Appleby replaced the computer lab's technology aide with a certified teacher. In the first year, the new technology teacher committed to working with classroom teachers to coordinate lab activities with classroom curriculum. Over the next two years, the technology teacher led classroom teachers to develop technology skills, evaluate software and techniques, and explore theme-based projects that used technology. Finally, teachers designed technology-rich projects of their own, fully integrated with the curriculum. After the third year, teachers continued to learn and apply technology as part of their ongoing professional development.

Student Involvement

Technology-savvy teachers are not the only resources a school can draw on for staff development for technology integration. Many students are also experts in some aspects of technology use. The "Generation www.Y" phenomenon recognizes that students are facile with technology and can provide help with troubleshooting and just-in-time technical assistance (Harper, Conor, and Course, 1999). The increased level of support made possible by student helpers can be a boon to teachers who are just learning to use technology in the classroom. Teachers can count on student experts to get a printer working, find a forgotten menu item, or answer an unexpected technical question that arises during instruction.

Nonetheless, as Harper, Conor, and Course (1999) point out, the student mentor approach is based on the premise that "it is not necessary to train teachers to be proficient with technology" (p. 7). Instead, students and teachers together create technology-infused lessons. Students give ongoing support, while teachers are responsible for pedagogy.

A very different approach to student involvement is the "Teacher Leader, Student Mentor" model created by Margo Greenhow, a reading specialist for the Dennis-Yarmouth, Massachusetts, schools. Greenhow applied for a state-level grant designed to jump-start the integration of technology throughout her school. The plan leveraged the school's strong, well-established program in writing across the curriculum and called for a semester-long staff development effort to prepare grade-level teacher leaders and selected students from each classroom to use innovative technology in the writing process. Guided by a technology specialist, teacher leaders explored several programs for writing. The teacher leaders worked with their grade-level peers to identify two capable students from every classroom and held several training sessions to prepare these students to use the same technologies. Meanwhile, Greenhow engaged all teachers in the school in planning a schoolwide writing project that would be shared with the community.

Once the lead teachers had readied their student technology experts, classroom teachers had all students participate in writing activities that used the new technologies and resulted in stories, poems, and essays for possible inclusion in a schoolwide publication. The final product, "Voices of Leadership," was distributed throughout the town and resulted in an increased level of commitment to technology for the district (Greenhow, 1996).

In this example of student involvement, students learned about teaching and about taking a responsible role in the learning activities of their peers. The student mentors had prestige, and they developed self-awareness and pride in their roles. The lead teachers were challenged by the task of training these bright youngsters, and typically they learned more from the students about technology in the process.

Ultimately the goal was for every teacher and every student to use technology in support of student writing, a goal that was achieved. Although a few teachers abdicated responsibility for use of technology, letting the student mentors and an instructional aide do all of the technical work, on the whole the experience engendered a sense of technology as a shared resource. It carried the expectation that all students would benefit and that all teachers would participate. Follow-on grants within the district have successfully used the same "teacher leader, student mentor" approach to technology infusion.

Teacher Leadership and Student Technology Competencies

Systemic integration of technology requires a district to define student technology competencies (STCs) for all subjects at all levels, as part of its technology plan. Recently the International Society for Technology in Education (ISTE) published the National Education Technology Standards (NETS), a model for these competencies (International Society for Technology in Education, 2000a). Determining how a district will adopt the standards across the curriculum and across grade levels is a significant effort that involves experienced teachers working collaboratively. Coughlin (1999) describes it this way: "Bringing technology-enriched opportunities to students . . . requires that schools be intentional in their implementation of technology, that they have clear and defensible student learning goals that they will support through a specific and well-designed use of educational technology" (p. 23).

Toward this end, districts may create teams of teachers to lead the effort to map standards to local curriculum and classroom practice. These teacher leaders need not be the most technology-savvy educators in the district. As Bray (1999) explains, "The team you create should have representation from all academic areas and grade levels who can design a vision of technology integration that will lead to attainable goals" (p. 15). Supporting such a team in a manner that leads to widescale adoption of technology-infused curriculum is no small undertaking, as the following example illustrates.

In the Shirley, Massachusetts, School District, nine teachers in the K–8 district were willing and able to take the lead with defining STCs and mapping them to the curriculum. However, they had little support for this formidable task: no common planning time, no release time, no stipends, and only limited funds to reimburse course work. At the same time, they were sensitive to their peers, knowing how complex it is for teachers who have no computer experience to learn and apply technology. With the help of a technology specialist, the district applied for and received a Technology Literacy Challenge Grant to assist with the effort. A year-long staff development program was fashioned around these teacher leaders with the aim of defining STCs across the curriculum and developing materials for classroom application that all teachers, regardless of technical skill level, could use.

After exploring a variety of approaches to technology integration, the teachers favored the development of well-designed cross-curricular projects at each grade level. Such projects fit well with the school's growing emphasis on high-order thinking, collaborative groups, individual responsibility, and authentic assessment.

The technology specialist believed that the goals established by the teacher leaders fit well with the growing practice of WebQuests (Yoder, 1999), which are curriculum-centered Internet research projects keyed to specific learning intentions. WebQuests had the advantage, once they had been developed and tested, of being easy to use by teachers who did not have much experience with technology.

Teacher leaders and the specialist met in intensive, hands-on sessions to identify curriculum units for WebQuest integration, pose challenging questions for students to pursue, find and critique resources, and test one another's projects. An important part of the discussion at each session was how the projects mapped to the curriculum and the STCs. As a corollary, during the development of the WebQuests, the teacher leaders learned many of the skills they wanted to foster in their students: purposeful and productive searching, critical evaluation of information, synthesis of divergent points of view, and presentation of key ideas. The group of teacher leaders produced a library of WebQuests for the school and then instructed their peers in how to incorporate the projects in their classrooms (Collier, 1999).

Inquiry and Action Research for Technology Integration

Designing and developing technology-integrated projects and units is not the end of the story. Assessing how well these units work in practice is an important step in effective, wide-scale technology integration. Inquiry and action research are important tools in this effort. Sparks and Loucks-Horsley (1989) note that "inquiry reflects a basic belief in teachers' ability to formulate valid questions about their own practice and to pursue objective answers to those questions" (p. 15). Action research that focuses on student learning can provide valuable insights concerning both technology integration and the curriculum and classroom practices already in place in a school.

Painter (2000) describes a successful experience with the "teacher as researcher" approach to staff development for technology integration. At the Deer Park Elementary School in Fairfax County, Virginia, teachers systematically studied the use of multimedia for student research presentations. Teacher researchers found that students enjoyed their collaborative projects and felt their work using multimedia was more creative than traditional approaches to reporting.

The findings of the teacher researchers went beyond these insights, however. They also found that they needed to strengthen the student research experience in a number of important ways: providing formal instruction in keyboarding, guided research, and structured note taking. Teachers also recognized the value of rubrics as an assessment tool, and they learned more about creating successful student research teams for collaborative projects. The lessons superseded effective use of technology and affected curriculum in the classroom, the library, and the technology program.

Technology consultant Jamie McKenzie favors such an inquiry approach to staff development for technology integration. In a collection of essays (1999), he describes the use of study groups to explore and establish the integration of technology in the curriculum. McKenzie's study groups make liberal use of internal and external resources as they explore ways to integrate technology for student learning. Their investigation springs from curiosity and deeply held beliefs about teaching and learning. The work of the study group focuses more on student learning than on technology and is dedicated to classroom action. Work done by the study group is reported periodically to administration for information and planning purposes.

Administrative Role

Each of the four approaches underscores the need for strong administrative support to make possible a complex aspect of systemic change: staff development for integration of technology in the curriculum. Administrators at the building level and in the central office are the planners who set the timetable and support the opportunities for staff development in the following ways:

- Establishing expectations and standards for accountability
- Adjusting priorities
- Encouraging assessment of technology use in the classroom, in the context of overall student achievement
- Providing incentives for exploratory application of technology, ensuring that such efforts are focused on curriculum and designed in a way that wide-scale implementation is a likely outcome
- Developing their own awareness of technology for learning and exercising their understanding in communication with teachers and staff
- Advocating for critical, ongoing technical support in the form of hardware maintenance and upgrades, personnel for technical support in the classroom, system-wide infrastructure, and a working technology plan

Resources for Staff Development and Technology Integration

At the national level, standards exist for student technology competencies (International Society for Technology in Education, 2000a) and teacher technology competency (National Council for Accreditation of Teacher Education, 1997; International Society for Technology in Education, 2000b). These can serve as guides for specifying local standards for student achievement, technology integration, and staff development.

Professional publications are excellent sources for exemplary lessons, projects, and technology-rich units of study. These include *Learning and Leading with Technology* (International Society for Technology in Education), *Technology and Learning* (Scholastic), *Classroom Connect*, and the *Curriculum/Technology Quarterly* (Association for Supervision and Curriculum Development).

Materials specifically developed to support staff development are available from the Association for Supervision and Curriculum

Development in the form of videos and packages; from publications such as *Classroom Connect*; and from software vendors such as Tom Snyder Productions. The ISTE/NETS book, *National Education Technology Standards for Students: Connecting Curriculum and Technology* (2000a), is a treasure trove of exemplary lesson plans linked to student technology competencies at all grade levels.

The Association for Supervision and Curriculum Development publishes several handbooks that guide action research in the school, including Calhoun's *How to Use Action Research in the Self-Renewing School* (1994).

Finally, on-line resources are invaluable for teachers in selecting software, including the *California Instructional Technology Clearing-house* (California Department of Education, 1998), and integrating Internet sites for student use, including *The WebQuest Page* (http://edweb.sdsu.edu/webquest/webquest.html) and Kathy Schrock's *Guide for Educators* (http://discoveryschool.com/schrockguide/).

References

Bray, B. "Eight Steps to Success: Technology Staff Development That Works." *Learning and Leading with Technology*, 1999, *27*(3), 14–20.

Breithaupt, D. "Collaborative Curriculum Development: Computer Education for Pre-service and In-service Teachers." [http://www.coe.uh.edu/insite/elec_pub/HTML1998/td_brei.htm]. 1998.

California Department of Education. *California Instructional Technology Clearinghouse*. [http://clearinghouse.k12.ca.us/]. 1998.

Calhoun, E. F. *How to Use Action Research in the Self-Renewing School*. Alexandria, Va.: Association for Supervision and Curriculum Development, 1994.

Collier, C. "Project-Based Student Technology Competencies." *Learning and Leading with Technology*, 1999, *27*(3), 50–54.

Coughlin, E. "Professional Competencies for the Digital Age Classroom." *Learning and Leading with Technology*, 1999, *27*(3), 22–27.

Grant, C. M. "Professional Development in a Technological Age: New Definitions, Old Challenges, New Resources." [http://ra.terc.edu/alliance/TEMPLATE/alliance_resources/reform/tech-infusion/prof_dev/prof_dev_frame.html]. 1996.

Greenhow, M. "Writing—Voices of Leadership." Unpublished grant proposal, Massachusetts Department of Education, Fund Code 508 Gifted and Talented, 1996.

Guskey, T. (ed.). *ASCD Yearbook 1998: Learning and Technology*. Alexandria, Va.: Association for Supervision and Curriculum Development, 1998.

Harper, D., Conor, J., and Course, A. "Why Generation www.Y?" *Learning and Leading with Technology*, 1999, *27*(2), 6–9.

International Society for Technology in Education. *National Education Technology Standards for Students: Connecting Curriculum and Technology*. Eugene, Ore.: International Society for Technology in Education, 2000a.

International Society for Technology in Education. *National Education Technology Standards for Teachers*. Eugene, Ore.: International Society for Technology in Education, 2000b. [http://cnets.iste.org/index3.html].

Katzenmeyer, M., and Moller, G. *Awakening the Sleeping Giant: Leadership Development for Teachers*. Thousand Oaks, Calif.: Corwin Press. 1996.

Little, J. W. "Norms of Collegiality and Experimentation: Workplace Conditions of School Success." *American Educational Research Journal*, 1982, *19*(3), 325–340.

McKenzie, J. *How Teachers Learn Technology Best*. Bellingham, Wash.: FNO Press. 1999.

National Council for Accreditation of Teacher Education. *Technology and the New Professional Teacher: Preparing for the 21st Century Classroom*. [http://www.ncate.org/accred/projects/tech/tech-21.htm]. 1997.

Office of Technology Assessment. *Teachers and Technology: Making the Connection*. Washington, D.C.: Office of Technology Assessment, 1995.

Painter, D. "Teacher as Researcher: A Means to Assess the Effectiveness of Technology in the Classroom." *Learning and Leading with Technology*, 2000, *27*(7), 10–13, 27.

Sherwood, S. "From Computer Lab to Technology Class: A Formula for Transformation." *Learning and Leading with Technology*, 1999, *27*(3), 28–31.

Sparks, D., and Loucks-Horsley, S. "Five Models of Staff Development for Teachers." *Journal of Staff Development*, 1989, *10*(4), 40–57.

Yoder, M. B. "The Student WebQuest." *Learning and Leading with Technology*, 1999, *26*(7), 7–9, 52–53.

Chapter Six

International On-Line Learning

Cultural Issues for Educators

Jyrki Pulkkinen, Merja Ruotsalainen

A cooperative on-line learning environment that simultaneously served diverse cultures and supported multiple approaches to study in several countries both provided benefits and posed difficulties.

The international on-line university course for teachers described in this chapter operates in an environment that stresses the student's own activity and the student's cooperation in a learning community. The course design is based on theories of learning, culture, and technology. The course evaluation findings show that the greatest problems in carrying out a course of this nature are existing student and tutor study expectations, technical problems in carrying out the course, and dissimilarities in learning and teaching cultures across national boundaries. These phenomena are seen in the insufficiency of the students' prior study skills and of the tutors' and teachers' guidance skills. Most notable among these is the deficiency of the skills of self-direction among students.

Distributed Learning in an International Context

Since 1996, the Faculty of Education at the University of Oulu has been offering Web-based on-line courses for preservice and inservice teachers inside and outside Finland. One particular course,

"Lego/Logo Construction Kit as a Learning Environment in Technology Education (Lego Dacta)," has undergone several stages of development. The Lego/Logo Construction Kit is a mechanical device that can be created from Lego pieces and is often motorized. Its actions can be launched from remote locations on a computer network, such as the Internet, and therefore is well-suited to distributed learning techniques. (The Web site for this course is found at http://edtech.oulu.fi/t3/courses/wp13/.) A draft version of the course was offered in autumn 1996 to preservice student teachers at the University of Oulu in northern Finland. In spring 1997 and 1998, international Lego Dacta courses were added in English for non-Finnish European student teachers. The two major goals of the course are to introduce some key questions in control technology (especially the Lego Dacta Construction Kit) as a part of the technology education and to compare differences and similarities in different European cultures.

This course is part of a European Union (EU)–funded project, Telematics for Teacher Training (T3), in which the University of Oulu is a full participant. The University of Exeter in the United Kingdom (http://telematics.ex.ac.uk/T3/) heads the T3 project, which encourages teachers to adopt telecommunications, new technologies, and restructured ways of working in schools and universities across the EU (Lam, Taconis, and Veen, 1997). The trial Lego/Logo course of 1996–1997 provided the data for this chapter.

Theoretical Background

The Lego Dacta course explicitly promotes student-centered study that stresses the student's own activity and cooperation. According to Gokhale (1995), collaborative methods of study develop students' critical thinking and direct them toward the construction of their own knowledge through discussion, clarification of their own thinking, and evaluation of their peers' ideas. The basic idea of a constructive learning psychology is that the students themselves construct their knowledge and skills through their own scaffolded

experiences (Salomon and Perkins, 1996). Such learning best occurs in situations and environments arranged for this purpose,
putting emphasis on process goals and making sure that support
and guidance are available for learning (Järvelä, 1996).

In order to be effective, complex technology-centered learning
environments should take into account the following important
learning characteristics (Cennamo, Abell, and Chung, 1996):

- Students require ample experience with the material to
  be learned.
- Learners should be encouraged to concentrate on different
  types of tasks in their studies.
- Learning is an ongoing process, not simply an end in its
  own right.
- Learning is a social event

This suggests that course content should not be designed iden-
tically for all students, since each student must be able to adapt the
course to fit individual experiences and goals. Courses such as this
must also offer alternative approaches to study and the potential
for students to proceed according to their particular interests and
abilities.

The constructivist notions underlying the open learning characteristics of the course are closely aligned with thinking about the
nature of knowledge in the teaching and learning process. Knowledge is an important aim of learning, but the nature of knowledge
is dependent on the "knower's" point of view. It is essential for the
researcher of learning environments to think about the nature of
knowledge and its relation to the various elements of the learning
environment under development.

Wilson (1995) discusses the relationship between the knowledge that underlies teaching and the nature of the learning environment that supports teaching. The learning materials, physical
objects, and information technology as vehicles of information do

not really reflect the most essential elements in a learning environment. Rather, learning requires enculturation and adaptation to a group's ways of seeing and acting. Knowledge is constructed socially; therefore, the overall nature of learning cannot be explained simply by the subjective experiences of individuals or by "objective facts," even if it is partly dependent on them.

Elements of Technology-Backed Constructivist Learning Environments

Figure 6.1 presents the three elements that sustain all of the telematics courses offered by the University of Oulu Educational Technology Research Unit: learning theories, the technology employed to implement the course, and a culture for production and collaboration in the learning community. The model is based on development work that has been in progress for several years (Pulkkinen and Niemi, 1996). A particular result of this work is the Project Tools for Learning (ProTo) learning environment that makes use of Web technology to author courses and teach them according to the constructivist principles discussed above. ProTo consists of a remote editor to produce the project pages easily on the Web and special discussion forums for reflective conversation.

The elements necessary for learning are built on these cornerstones. These elements can be illustrated more fully in terms of pedagogical functions, appropriate technologies, and social organization of learning.

Pedagogical Functions

Pedagogical functions flow from activities and methods in the learning environment that make learning possible. In the ProTo model, the following basic functions are present in the learning environment. Learning activities consist of collaboration and self-directed study. Students develop goal-oriented project documents

Figure 6.1. Elements of an Open Learning Environment.

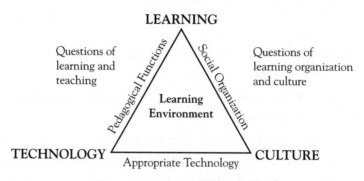

and present them to peers on Web pages authored within ProTo. They can have a variety of formats:

- Learning materials and experiments that offer background information about the course content
- Teaching situations that can be either live videoconferencing sessions or Web-based discussions
- Discussion forums, based on the ProTo application and managed by the course tutors that provide scaffolding and support for student learning
- Evaluation activities that consist of peer and tutor assessment of student work

Appropriate Technologies

Interactivity is the most important feature of modern digital technology that establishes the student interface in the virtual space of an open learning environment. In the Lego Dacta course, where the Web is the primary interface, there are three basic types of interactivity:

- Networked communication, orchestrated by the ProTo learning environment
- Remote interaction with Lego/Logo lab materials and hypertext learning materials
- Interactive synchronous integrated services digital network videoconferencing sessions, where students interact, face-to-face, with peers and tutors to raise and resolve issues related to their course experience

Social Organization of Learning

On-line university courses, whereby students and teachers come from different venues, require a distribution of the knowledge and skills embedded in the goals of a course. This must occur throughout a learning community that contains many different local learning cultures. However, a technically functional learning environment that may be fully justified in terms of learning psychology and modern technology can be rendered futile by students or teachers who bring different or opposing local expectations to the common environment (Pulkkinen and Niemi, 1996).

Evaluation Methodology for the Lego Dacta Course

According to Patton (1980), effective program evaluation demands the systematic collection, analysis, and interpretation of data on the functions and results of an educational project, so that others may assess the relative merits of its essential features for replication and future design. This evaluation examines the Lego Dacta course process as a case study. The methodological approach in this evaluation is eclectic, combining both quantitative and qualitative methods. An effort is made to triangulate evaluative data by using various research methods in a multifaceted way. The data, and the methodologies used to evaluate them, are intended to complement and validate each other. The evaluation of the Lego Dacta course is intended to improve and refine its design and implementation and to apply the results for future development within and beyond the T3 consortium.

For this project, research data were gathered in the following ways:

- From students by an on-line questionnaire
- From the tutors and teachers by asking them to write about their own experiences and provide informal feedback on the course
- By analyzing the project papers and discussions in the ProTo learning environment

The data contained both qualitative and quantitative items and were divided into three categories of evaluation results: pedagogical functionality, cultural acceptability and communicativeness, and technical design and reliability.

Forty-eight Finnish students participated in the original pilot course. These students were enrolled in either the University of Oulu educational technology specialist program or the technology-oriented primary teacher program. The students in the international follow-up course were seven technology teacher education students from the Netherlands, ten mature design and technology teacher education students from the United Kingdom, and one professional educator from Italy.

All of the students had been using computers prior to participating in this course for basic purposes such as word processing. There were differences among the various groups in other computer applications, such as the use of the different Internet services. Most of the Finnish students had browsed the Web before the course, while only a few of the Dutch and English students reported having done so.

Pedagogical Evaluation Results

In the student evaluation of this course, comments centered substantially on the ambiguities arising from an unfamiliarity with study in on-line flexible learning environments. Higher-order peer collaboration across national boundaries failed to materialize as hoped, reflecting a finding reported in a different course (LeBaron, Pulkkinen, and Scollin, 2000).

General Pedagogical Functionality

The students reporting on both the Finnish and international versions indicated that it was somewhat interesting, partly because of its novelty. The course content, method of study, and learning environment were new to them. However, the scheduling of the Finnish pilot course failed to take sufficient account of the students' timetables. This, combined with paucity of initial course information, appeared to reduce student interest.

Feedback from students in the international course was surprisingly positive considering the problems described by the teaching assistant tutors regarding scheduling, course progress, and technical functions of the environment. In general, openness of time and geography in the distributed learning environment and student-centered learning methods seemed to suit different students differently. Some of the students felt that the openness was challenging and motivating, while others indicated confusion resulting from the openness and unfamiliar demands on their own activity.

Specific Learning Activities

Most of the students indicated that the study method of working on a project paper in a Web learning environment generally suited them to varying degrees of satisfaction, although they found it difficult to select topics for study. In the Finnish pilot course, most of the students worked on their projects in small groups and felt that the content of their work was important.

Feedback from the students in the international course, however, demonstrated that the students did not know what was expected from them, and it was difficult for them to grasp the idea of a Web-based project paper. The unfamiliar "degrees of freedom" to study and interact at times of the students' choosing connected with project-based study created problems for some of the students in both groups. They felt that the challenges of choosing project topics and working independently were difficult. Thus, it seems important in courses like this to support the students who do not have the skills for self-directed study.

Particular Teaching Situations

The contents of the introductory lecture were considered quite poor in both courses. The insufficiency of initial information interfered with a successful course launch for some of the students. Even after the lecture, several reported difficulty in accessing the course content and initiating study based on available content. The student confusion regarding course information might have been associated with the pilot nature of the course. Students, tutors, and teachers may have been embarrassed in a situation that was new to them.

Learning Materials and Virtual "Laboratory" Experiments

Student responses to questions about the learning materials and the Lego/Logo virtual lab produced a variety of perspectives. The lack of study time reported by the students resulted in insufficient time to become adequately familiar with the course information and materials on the Web. This problem was found particularly in the international course. Although the Web materials were important from the viewpoint of the course content, it appears that the students had become only superficially familiar with them due to the lack of time and the inconvenience to their work schedules.

Tutoring

It appears that the students received a significant amount of course information through tutoring. They indicated that both personal and group tutoring in content matters supported and suited them well. Student feedback appears to show that in a course like Lego Dacta, which so strongly emphasizes autonomous methods of study, students do not necessarily know how to seek help when they encounter problems. This highlights the crucial role of effective, accessible tutoring. Participants in the international course placed special emphasis on this course feature.

Peer Collaboration

The students indicated that peer discussion is a good method of study. In practice, however, the students provided very little feedback to their peers. The nature of peer discussion failed to argue the knowledge that was originally the target of discussions. Much of the discussion concentrated on lower-order matters, consisting mostly of asking and giving the kind of practical advice that the tutors were expected to handle. In this sense, the goals set for knowledge validation and reflective thinking in the pilot course were not achieved.

When the students' documents were examined, about half of the project topics in the international course focused on control technology and Lego/Logo or on distance learning and the Internet. The remaining international students and most of those in the Finnish course had understood that the course was about the pedagogical applications of Lego/Logo in particular.

This finding might lead to the conclusion that it is much more difficult to maintain a disciplined content focus in international courses than it is for domestic students. This may be due partly to cultural and linguistic differences across national student groups. In a pilot course, where the content, study methods, and learning environment are new, it can also be difficult to limit study to the original content goals, since the environment and learning method may also become contents of study.

Evaluation of the Learning Culture

The open and independent study methods in this course did not mesh comfortably with the methods of study that the students had used previously. Student autonomy, networked communication, project-based study, and learner centeredness were new and strange to most of them. In addition, the students believed that the course was poorly integrated with the schedules of their other studies. In particular, the international course participants cited problems with their timetables. During the course, for example, the English students confronted major exams in their local studies. In Finland, graduate courses rarely have final exams, but in the United Kingdom, final exams are much more common. These exams for the British students conflicted with the project-based demands of work in one on-line course.

Many students did not know how to schedule their own studies outside the prearranged contact teaching sessions. Project-based open learning demands that students be capable of planning their own independent work. Questionnaire results indicate that students judged their own influence on course planning to have been quite small.

Confirming the questionnaire results, most of the tutors indicated that students encountered the greatest difficulty with independent goal setting and self-directed work. The old models of coaching that the tutors knew well could not be applied to the new situation, since not even they were knowledgeable about telematic distance learning. Thus, the open and flexible working methods of study also made new demands on the tutors. Some of the tutors felt insecure in their unfamiliar assignments. Because working in telematic learning environments was as unfamiliar to some of the tutors as it was to the students, it seems important to arrange special training for them before they are expected to provide support to their students.

Evaluation of Technical Design and Reliability

The ProTo learning environment was deemed quite easy to use. The students praised the ease of writing and reading in the ProTo discussion forum and on the Web pages generated by the students. The visual clarity of the laboratory's Web pages and the Web environment as a whole was considered good, indicating that the hypertext tools were acceptable for productive student activity.

Student activity in this course was made difficult, however, by technical problems not only in the Lego/Logo lab but also in some international Internet connections and the local technical equipment. Notwithstanding this difficulty, the reliability of the local computers and Internet connections was considered relatively good. The poor technical reliability of the Lego/Logo laboratory was attributable partly to its experimental nature, causing student frustration and decreased motivation. Therefore, the Lego/Logo lab was used relatively little.

Conclusion

The greatest problem in this telematic course, especially the international version, seemed to be the gulf in learning and teaching culture between open and flexible networked environments and traditional practice. This is seen in the underdevelopment of students' study skills and the tutors' and teachers' guidance skills in telematic learning environments. The major problem is cultural—not so much in a national or ethnic sense as in expectations about learning and teaching. Despite the many practical problems, teachers, tutors, and students felt that independent, open, and flexible distance learning made sense in principle. Most of the students signaled a willingness to participate in similar future courses if the shortcomings they identified were corrected. Although the ProTo application was thought to be quite easy to use, there remains a need for features that help students structure their learning activities better, leading them to deeper understanding and reflection in the learning process. Of course, the technical problems related to the virtual lab need to be remedied.

Some of the major problems dealing with open and flexible distance-learning courses were due to the difficulties in integrating these courses with the students' and teachers' existing work requirements. To ensure that telematic courses are not disconnected from the real lives of their constituents, the curriculum and organization should be sufficiently flexible to accommodate integration with other aspects of the students' study or work.

In addition to the notion that the pedagogical ideas of a telematic course should be made clear to the students and the tutors, students and tutors should also be introduced to the unfamiliar requirements of new learning cultures before they are immersed in the pressures of a real course. It is not enough simply to increase the share of telematics and distance education in the overall curriculum; much advance preparation and organization is also required.

References

Cennamo, K. S., Abell, S. K., and Chung, M-L. "A 'Layers of Negotiation' Model for Designing Constructivist Learning Materials." *Educational Technology*, 1996, 36(4), 39–48.

Gokhale, A. A. "Collaborative Learning Enhances Critical Thinking." *Journal of Technology Education*, 1995, 7(1), 22–30. [http://scholar.lib.vt.edu/ejournals/JTE/v7nl/gokhale.jte-v7nl.html].

Järvelä, S. *Cognitive Apprenticeship Model in a Complex Technology-based Learning Environment.* University of Joensuu, 1996.

Lam, I., Taconis, R., and Veen, W. "An Interactive Virtual Workshop: A Potential Tool in Teacher Training?" Paper presented at the CAL 97 Conference,

University of Exeter, United Kingdom, Mar. 23–26, 1997. [http://www.media.uwe.ac.uk/~masoud/cal-97/papers/lam-3.htm].

LeBaron, J., Palkkinen, J., and Scollin, P. "Promoting Cross-Border Communication in an International Web-Based Graduate Course." *Interactive Multimedia Electronic Journal of Computer-Enhanced Learning,* 2000, 2(2). [http://imej.wfu.edu/articles/2000/2/01/index.asp].

Patton, M. *Qualitative Evaluation Methods.* Thousand Oaks, Calif.: Sage, 1980.

Pulkkinen, J., and Niemi, E. "Multimedia and New Models of Learning in the Internet." In V.W.S. Chow (ed.), *Multimedia Technology and Applications.* New York: Springer-Verlag, 1996.

Salomon, G., and Perkins, D. "Learning in Wonderland: What Do Computers Really Offer Education?" In S. T. Kerr (ed.), *Technology and the Future of Schooling: Ninety-Fifth Yearbook of the National Society for the Study of Education.* Part II. Chicago: University of Chicago Press, 1996.

Wilson, B. G. "Metaphors for Instruction: Why We Talk About Learning Environments." *Educational Technology,* 1995, 35(5).

Chapter Seven

The Computers Are Here!

Now What Does the Principal Do?

George S. Perry Jr., Ronald J. Areglado

Technology-supported curricular transformation
demands visionary leadership and effective
management from school principals.

Principals have worked tirelessly to bring computers and other technologies to their schools. Technology labs filled with excited students learning with the latest software are sources of pride and
accomplishment for schools and their principals and are among the
first stops on a school tour. Unfortunately, the technology lab is usually the last place on the tour a visitor will actually see technology
used in teaching and learning. Computers are often located far from
classrooms, where most teaching and learning take place. The distance between the technology lab and the classroom symbolizes the
distance between technology-enriched instruction and technology-
devoid instruction. The fact is that investments in equipment have
not always been accompanied by changes in teaching.

Each school's experience with technology is different. Most
schools and teachers we know struggle to use technology. Even
teachers comfortable with technology face obstacles in integrating
it into their instruction for reasons that are operational, instructional, or practical (Cuban, 1999). Leadership by the principal is
necessary to help teachers overcome obstacles and integrate technology into their instructional practice. Principals' work in leading their school in technology continues, rather than ends, when

computers are unboxed, installed, and networked. They must plan for and think about the technology needs of adults if technology is to become a leading instructional tool.

What Does Leadership Mean?

Traditionally principals have been seen as managers responsible for implementing district policies and directives in schools (Morris, Crowson, Porter-Gehrie and Hurwitz, 1984). During the 1990s, however, principals were expected to add leadership to their roles as managers (Beck and Murphy, 1993). Research has distinguished between leaders and managers. Zaleznick (1977) argues that managers focus on improving the operations of their organizations. Managers are described as

- Tough-minded problem solvers
- Dedicated task completors
- Compromisers
- Bureaucrats
- Protectors of the existing order of affairs

Managers believe that "if it ain't broke, don't fix it."

Good management maintains and perpetuates a school. Teachers, support staff, students, parents, and community groups look to the principal to administer the innumerable daily operations of the school. To manage efficient operations, principals must do many things right. Doing things right, however, is not necessarily leadership.

Zaleznick suggests that leaders have different skills and perspectives. Leaders focus on creating new approaches and imagining new visions. They:

- Have personal and active attitudes toward goals
- Develop fresh approaches to long-standing problems
- Are comfortable with high levels of risk

- Are intuitive and empathic, thinking about what events and decisions mean to participants
- Create turbulence to intensify motivation and produce unintentional outcomes

Leaders believe that when it "ain't broke may be the only time you can fix it."

Leadership is necessary to move the school in new and fundamentally different directions. Instructional questions offer principals their greatest opportunity to lead. Such questions include "What is essential for students to know and be able to do?" and "What constitutes good instruction?" The answers to such questions help define a school's purpose. Leading means helping teachers understand the need to change, value the changes that will take place, and change their own beliefs and practices. It results in helping teachers replace their good practice with better practice.

Management and leadership are different. Some principals are predisposed to be managers, while others are inclined to leadership. Increasingly, principals need to serve effectively as both leaders and managers and to encourage teachers to exercise leadership and management within their schools.

Instructional Leadership

With the heightened national interest in improved student performance, high-stakes testing, and school accountability, the principal's role as the school's instructional leader has become more significant. Rutherford (1985) notes that effective principals have clear and informed visions of what they want their schools to become—visions that focus on students and their needs; translate these visions into goals for their schools and expectations for their teachers, students, and other administrators; monitor progress continuously; and intervene in a supportive or corrective manner when necessary.

Effective leadership among principals seems to influence student performance. Andrews, Soder, and Jacoby (1986) report that the

Principals can apply data gleaned from considering these factors in deciding what kinds of individual adult learning would best meet the school's needs. Individual learning opportunities may not be the most appropriate, however. Principals may instead determine that interventions for the entire school are more appropriate. In this situation, Hart suggests that principals concentrate on three group capacity factors:

- The culture of the school to determine group norms
- The processes principals and teachers use to communicate and make sense of objective information
- Organizational self-study and improvement processes focusing explicitly on changes in structures, procedures, and norms

These group factors provide data on a school's readiness to be a learning organization. In reviewing the data, principals and other professional development leaders might determine that the school is not yet ready to move to building-wide learning and may choose to emphasize individual learning or implement other intermediate steps.

Leading Change for Technology Integration

The change process that principals use has more impact on the success or failure of an innovation than the innovation itself (Sarason, 1996). Principals are at the center of the change process. It is not that they can ensure that change will happen, but they can prevent it from happening by not having an effective change process (Evans, 1996; Fullan, 1991). Kotter (1996) introduces an eight-step developmental change process that we have found particularly appropriate for overcoming the complex factors contributing to individual and group resistance to technological change. The process relies on high-quality leadership and excellent management from not only the principal but also others from the school.

Step 1: Establishing a Sense of Urgency

People need a reason to change, and whole school change is sustained by a shared sense of urgency. Kotter suggests that there are many ways in which "doing business as usual" sends implicit and explicit messages that reinforce complacency and resistance to change. Creating a sense of urgency means developing a rationale for transformation that is powerful enough to capture the attention of staff and send consistent signals of an urgent need for change. There are ways in which teachers can be helped to see that integrating technology responds to real threats facing the school or students. Kotter suggests that unless all of senior management (principals and their assistants) and at least 75 percent of middle management (department heads, lead teachers) and the majority of employees are convinced that change is important, the process will not be sustained.

Step 2: Creating a Guiding Coalition

By themselves, principals cannot create, lead, or sustain change. Kotter calls the group that should direct change the "guiding coalition." Members of the guiding coalition are selected initially by the principal based on position, interest, expertise, credibility, and leadership. In selecting coalition members, the principal considers the following factors:

Position power. Are enough key players on board, especially opinion leaders, so that those who are left out cannot easily block progress? Are formal (such as union leaders) and informal (such as vocal and resistant teachers) leaders included?

Expertise. Are the various points of view—teachers at different grade levels, administrators, support staff, parents, and students—adequately represented so that informed, intelligent decisions will be made?

Credibility. Does the coalition have enough people with good reputation so that its recommendations will be taken seriously by others?

Leadership. Does the coalition include enough proven leaders (such as those who can create vision) to drive the change process? Are leaders complemented by managers able to develop and implement plans?

The size of an effective coalition depends on the size of the school. The guiding coalition might start small and then add members over time. Once the members are identified, Kotter suggests that the coalition's first tasks are to build support and teamwork and identify a common goal. Although the principal may charge the coalition with integrating technology into classroom practice, the members, including the principal, will need to make meaning of the charge through the development of a common goal as a focal point for all members to achieve. (Chapter Two discusses the planning process for technology integration in greater detail.)

Step 3: Developing a Vision and a Strategy

Kotter defines *vision* as a picture of the future accompanied by a sense about why people should strive to create that future. The vision is supported by strategies for how it may be achieved. The broad, creative aspects of the strategies are primarily in the domain of skilled leaders. Visions need plans and budgets to be realized, and these are primarily in the domain of capable managers. Plans are specific steps and time lines to implement the strategies. Budgets are plans converted into resource parameters and goals.

Vision, strategies, plans, and budgets need to work in concert to be effective, as do the leaders and managers working on them. Teamwork and honest talk must exist if the conceptual and implementation errors are to be identified and solved. The strategies, plans, and budgets should be considered working drafts that are adjusted based on current information and better thinking.

Step 4: Communicating the Vision

The real power of the vision is unleashed when a critical mass of the people in the school have a common understanding of its goals and directions. The guiding coalition sifts through mountains of information on the way to digesting, understanding, and reaching decisions. Then the coalition communicates the shared vision in ways that stakeholders can understand and embrace.

Step 5: Empowering Employees for Broad-Based Action

In addition to communicating the vision to stakeholders, the coalition assumes responsibility for removing the obstacles to reaching the vision. Again, the coalition needs to think deeply about the potential structural obstacles:

- Availability and organization of time
- Student grouping
- Space and infrastructure needed to use technology effectively
- Training to support teacher transformation with technology
- Aligning information and personal systems (for example, ensuring teacher access to information about training and equipment and aligning teacher evaluation processes to reward demonstrations of technology skills)
- Confronting people in authority who block change (such as making sure that lead teachers, department heads, and assistant principals send consistent messages)

Step 6: Generating Short-Term Wins

Changing teaching practice is a long journey that can be sustained only by short-term successes. Short-term wins provide evidence that sacrifices are worth the effort, reward change agents for their contributions, help fine-tune vision and strategies, undermine cynics and self-serving resisters, keep people with authority and stakeholders on board, and build momentum. Short-term wins might include teacher and student technology demonstrations or celebration of fully networked classrooms. It is during this step that sustained change begins to occur. Transformation of teaching practice begins when teachers and students see that success is possible and the consequences rewarded. When this happens, the change process accelerates.

Step 7: Consolidating Gains to Produce Deeper Change

Celebrations of short-term wins are important but should be short-lived. Success spurs further opportunity and generates more work. The coalition applies the credibility from short-term wins to take on larger and deeper initiatives. Additional people are asked to join the effort, new strategies and plans are developed, and resisters are approached. Coalition leaders continue to focus on maintaining clarity of purpose and keeping urgency levels high. Managers eliminate short circuits to change. All members continue to reflect on, analyze, and restructure their efforts in the light of changing conditions.

Step 8: Anchoring Change in the Culture

The final step is to institutionalize change by recognizing, establishing, and reinforcing new norms of group and individual behavior. Kotter believes that a culture changes only after people's ways of acting have been altered, new behaviors have produced recognizable group benefit over time, and people see connections between the new actions and student performance. Stakeholders need to engage in perpetual conversation that is grounded in evidence that change is not only occurring but is serving the vision that drives it.

Conclusion

Systemic transformation is ill served by piecemeal tinkering. The first four steps of Kotter's change process are necessary preconditions to supporting and sustaining change. Attempts at changing teaching practice can result only from a long process, one that begins with a rationale for transformation that shows leadership by engaging key people in designing changes. The process is clear about its goals and directions and communicates the goals and directions before applying solutions.

Principals' leadership for technology transformation begins, rather than ends, when technology arrives at the school. Moving from installation to transformational use urges principals to be intentional, which requires an instructional vision and a strategy for implementation. Successful instructional transformation obliges principals to be actively involved in all aspects of the process. Active involvement allows principals to send the implicit and explicit messages that create a sense of urgency, guide the implementation strategy, and create change in the whole school. The principal's direct involvement does not ensure success, but its absence guarantees failure in the quest for improved instruction through technology.

References

Andrews, R., Soder, R. and Jacoby, D. "Principals' Roles, Student Achievement, and the Other School Variables." Paper presented at the Annual Meeting of the American Educational Research Association, San Francisco, 1986.

Beck, L. G., and Murphy, J. Understanding the Principalship: Metaphorical Themes, 1920s–1990s. New York: Teachers College Press, 1993.

Cuban, L. "The Technology Puzzle." Education Week, Aug. 4, 1999, p. 68.

Evans, R. The Human Side of School Change: Reform, Resistance, and the Real Life Problems of Innovation. San Francisco: Jossey-Bass, 1996.

Fullan, M., with Stiegelbauer, S. The New Meaning of Educational Change. (2nd ed.) New York: Teachers College Press, 1991.

Glickman, C. "Pretending Not to Know What We Know." Educational Leadership, 1991, 48(8), 4–10.

Hart, A. W. "Managing School Performance: The Role of the Administrator." In P. Reyes (ed.), *Teachers and Their Workplace*. Thousand Oaks, Calif.: Sage, 1990.

Kotter, J. P. *Leading Change*. Boston: Harvard Business School Press, 1996.

Little, J. W., and Bird, T. "Instructional Leadership: 'Close to the Classroom' in Secondary Schools." In W. Greenfield (ed.), *Instructional Leadership: Concepts, Issues and Controversies*. Needham Heights, Mass.: Allyn & Bacon, 1987.

Morris, V. C., Crowson, R. L., Porter-Gehrie, C., and Hurwitz, E., Jr. *Principals in Action: The Reality of Managing Schools*. Columbus, Ohio: Charles E. Merrill, 1984.

Rutherford, W. "School Principals as Effective Leaders." *Phi Delta Kappan*, 1985, 67, 31–34.

Sarason, S. B. *Revisiting the Culture of the School and the Problem of Change*. New York: Teachers College Press, 1996.

Smith, W., and Andrews, R. *Instructional Leadership: How Principals Make a Difference*. Alexandria, Va.: Association for Supervision and Curriculum Development, 1989.

Zaleznik, A. "Managers and Leaders: Are They Different?" *Harvard Business Review*, 1977, 55(3), 67–78.

Chapter Eight

Building Public Support

The Politics of Technology Transformation

Isa Kaftal Zimmerman

Improving teaching and learning through technology requires attention to politics as well as to pedagogy.

Half of the population knows exactly what you should do; the other half does not know what you are talking about. You need different strategies for different folks. So goes the story of technology in schools.

That public education increasingly involves all the public in its deliberations stems from the low esteem in which much of public education is held these days and from the technology itself. Everyone has easy access to school leaders through e-mail and the Web. Communications networks transform public interaction.

Public education on the local level is still an arena in which the public's wishes have some possibility of being accommodated. Nowhere is this clearer than in the politics of technology, where the list of stakeholders runs the gamut from the U.S. government to students. In the United States, former President Clinton and Vice President Gore supported the information highway. At the time, the director of the Office of Technology was a former teacher and a friend of public education. Pronouncements and funds from the federal level are messages to local educators that the issue of technology is important.

Who Is Involved in the Politics
of Technology Transformation?

The state government must be centrally engaged; wide area networking infrastructure cannot be developed by individual school districts. The key to engaging the state government is to marshal the forces of business and education to work together on a funding agenda (capital bond bills, annual budget line items, special appropriations) and a series of mandates. For example, school districts, as well as their state education agencies, should be required to submit multiyear technology plans in order to access any special matching monies from the state. Those plans should be updated annually, making the use of technology in schools part of any educational reform initiative. In Massachusetts, a number of activists formed an organization called Business and Education for Schools and Technology (BEST). The membership includes business collaboratives such as Associated Industries of Massachusetts and the Software Council, as well as the various professional educator associations.

A report by Hezel Associates (1998) claims that without a state governor's buy-in, technology does not get very far in any state. One of BEST's major accomplishments during its years of campaigning has been to garner the official support from the past and current Massachusetts governors.

Although one thinks globally, one must act locally. Education is a state obligation, but in most states, it is predominantly a local prerogative. So school committees, as they are called in Massachusetts, are responsible for establishing policies and securing annual funding from taxpayers. Educating school committees is essential to ensure a steady revenue stream for technology in the appropriated budget, in addition to whatever grants and gifts schools receive.

Parents and the rest of the community must support the cost of maintaining the technology program through voting for special warrant articles and the annual school budget. In our communities, we (the Acton and Acton-Boxborough, Massachusetts, school committees) tied networking to other essential needs by creating a single warrant article that included Americans with Disabilities Act requirements and health and safety items, so that technology would be difficult to vote down. We impressed the town meeting (an annual set of meetings in Massachusetts towns that all local voters may attend and cast their individual votes on issues relating to town matters) with our budget presentations using the computer, setting the standard for every other group that has come before the town meeting since then.

School administrators, especially principals, must take the lead by modeling and explaining the value of technology used appropriately in the classroom and the office. Teachers are the ultimate supporters because they must use the technology wisely with their students. They must integrate the technology into curriculum and instruction. And finally students have a role because once they understand the enhanced capacity provided by the technology, they will demand it in order to be prepared for their future.

During the first year of the two school systems' network, in 1995, high school students came forward to help. They created the Acton-Boxborough Internet Scout Service (ABISS) in order to teach teachers how to use the Internet and to search the Internet for material for their teachers' classes. A parallel group was formed at the same time in one of the elementary schools. One of the students created the first district Web page, and students and teachers supplied material for the site.

Many community organizations can play seminal roles. Colleges and universities can provide the research and evaluation that are badly needed to convince certain critical, and as yet unpersuaded, segments of the population. The chamber of commerce brings together businesses and schools to engage in mutually beneficial activities. Technology businesses partner with schools to offer expertise and in-kind support. Volunteer organizations spread the word about the educational utility of technology while offering support in and to the schools.

The schools themselves need to collaborate with other districts to maximize the potential for grants, professional development, and low-enrollment courses (Latin and advanced mathematics, for example) and to minimize unnecessary duplication. Some duplication will be inevitable. People learn by doing; they cannot simply learn from other people's experiences. With so many small school districts everywhere, each often reinventing the wheel, sharing information and experience as well as scarce resources can be highly useful to the entire enterprise.

How Can the Stakeholders Be Engaged and Activated?

Politics is about building support. Involving everyone and maintaining people's enthusiasm and a sense of urgency are critical. This task can seem overwhelming at times, but there are strategies that have proven valuable and successful.

Campaigning at the Grassroots

Establishing grassroots organizations such as BEST takes a few dedicated beginners with a little time and very little money (basically for postage and stationery). Using e-mail, the following grassroots strategies have been very effective:

- Identifying a person in each school district who will contact a state representative and senator when asked
- Keeping a list of the senators and representatives handy, with their e-mail addresses and telephone numbers (on paper or on the Web) so they can be easily advised
- Maintaining a Web site of current and correct information related to technology aspirations
- Using volunteer assistance and the facilities of friendly partners

These are all simple and effective techniques. Testifying before the legislature and writing letters and position papers are all necessary steps in the political process of electing a candidate for public office. They are equally powerful in moving the technology agenda ahead. (For a detailed account of BEST's operations and achievements, see Lowd, 1998.)

Creating coalitions outside the system through working with nonprofits, businesses, agencies, and user groups is another important step. In Massachusetts, we were able to convince the MITRE Corporation and the Massachusetts Business Roundtable to listen to the ideas and concerns of school superintendents. Prior to the existence of BEST, we created the Massachusetts Technology Collaborative (MTC) so that educators, public employees, and business and university representatives could meet regularly to think about the issues and plan the education of specific key groups. Businesspeople need particular attention. Often they do not give educators enough credit for their understanding. When we first started working with the president of the MITRE Corporation, he claimed that superintendents would "not know how to spend a million dollars" on technology.

Establishing a local community technology advisory committee (or CTAC, as we called our local groups), composed of community members, parents, school personnel, and sometimes students, gave us the legitimacy, energy, and expertise to move the agenda to the school committee and the town meeting levels. We asked them to focus on the networking piece of our technology plan. CTAC helped us to market our needs to the communities. We used our town cable TV show, articles and the superintendent's column in the local newspapers, letters to the editor, articles in the student high school newspaper, memos to the school committee (whose meetings are televised), and features in the school district newsletter. CTAC 2, now in operation, has expanded to advise on the deployment of computers, update the mission of technology in the schools, and provide technical assistance, an agenda unimaginable several years ago.

We mounted Tech Expo on a Sunday afternoon, showing off every use of technology then available in our school systems, calling on our business partners to demonstrate their initiatives and new products. In addition to the educative function, Tech Expo served as a community-building activity. The first occasion was followed by annual events until the base of support was established. Now the issue is less whether technology is necessary; rather, the issue is how much to spend and how to spend it.

The NetDay movement, which started in California, has become popular not only in the United States but also in Europe. On NetDay, teams of community volunteers actually went into schools to assist school personnel in wiring the buildings and installing computer network facilities. Massachusetts has developed arguably one of the best versions of NetDay; its broad coalition of stakeholders has included professional development and curriculum integration as part of the basic design. NetDays themselves were political events, with legislators highly visible at selected sites and in their own school districts. The planning process was educational and inclusionary. The collaborative that launched Massachusetts NetDay has become a significant provider of technological services to local schools. With the state's Department of Education, it has begun to develop a Web-based teaching-learning-administrative system for all teachers, students, administrators, and parents designed to enhance learning across the K–12 enterprise. It is called Virtual Education Space.

Supporting Change at the Grassroots

From the very beginning our two school systems made the use of technology a part of systemwide goals, which are reviewed and revised annually. These are then developed into school goals, keeping everyone informed. By virtue of state-promulgated performance criteria, the appropriate use of technology has also become part of the annual performance appraisal of school personnel. This means that every member of the school districts must pay attention to the use of technology.

None of the efforts to bring technology into schools can succeed without sufficient professional development for teachers and other staff. Equally important are models or pilots of appropriate uses and personnel to support teachers in their work. Many studies and papers—for example, the Milken report published by *Education Week* (1998) and the U.S. Office of Technology Assessment's national report (1995)—state the obvious: that by itself, technology does nothing significant for education. Technology must be used in accordance with a plan and supported by teachers who know how and when to use it, have sufficient access to it, can help students use it, have time to think about using it, and can fail in their first attempts to use it.

In the earlier days of educational technology, there were three waves of teachers: the risk-taking experimenters or pioneers and champions, those needing a little encouragement and support, and the "mighty resisters." (At a Tech Expo I attended during a heavy rainstorm, there was a momentary loss of power until the auxiliary generator kicked in. In the dark auditorium, while the cool presenter reorganized his technological presentation, the mathematics department head was heard to comment, "That's why I always carry chalk in my pocket!")

During these more primitive times, a district had to decide where to put its resources for the three waves. Now students must be technology savvy to make their way successfully after graduation. There are thousands of jobs waiting for people with technology training. It is therefore a greater challenge for schools to find sufficient personnel to provide all the training and curriculum development needed for everyone on staff.

The Role of the Media

We cannot minimize the influence of the media on any agenda, certainly not on the use of technology in schools. One news article or editorial with a negative story or comments by a key decision maker about educational technology has the potential to rally the unconvinced and can lead a school committee member to vote against the purchase of technology for the schools. An important strategy is to respond and set the record straight whenever necessary. In the 1980s, after Seymour Papert (1980) of MIT made his damning observation that schools were not using technology as fully as possible, it looked as if he had killed all political potential for technology investment. He has since changed his mind, but his prominent name in the media had a strongly negative effect on public opinion.

It is easy to be swayed by prevailing negative opinion. In the battle for technology in schools, standing firm while others are railing against the use of computers is essential. Following are some ways to do that:

- Have a vision—literally a picture in your head of what "it will look like when . . ."
- Develop a plan for the school district, other key players, and for yourself so that you can continue to encourage people.
- Know how the computers are being used and what students are learning by having the data at hand.
- Develop a group of colleagues with whom you can share problems and solutions.

If some of the players resist, you must insist. Later they may thank you. When I was a high school principal, I required the faculty to spend two hours "playing with computers." They were furious before—and enthralled and hooked after.

Educational leaders need to model the desired behaviors. They must use the technology themselves in the most visible ways possible. My most powerful early example was having a workstation on my desk and writing memos directly on the computer with other administrators as we spoke. Using e-mail to send urgent messages was another way to engage colleagues and lead by example.

Major Stakeholder Issues

Several issues beyond money issues need reconciliation among the stakeholders.

Demonstrating Efficacy.

In business, expending a great deal of money on technology without proof of success is a matter of course; this is not the case for public education. There is increasing research that shows that technology, when used properly, has a positive impact on student learning (Wenglinsky, 1998) by leading to improved writing skills, presentations, research, and higher-order thinking. The Milken report has documented several beneficial consequences of well-designed educational technology projects.

Some school districts conduct their own assessment. In the late 1980s, the Lexington, Massachusetts, district chose one school to determine the value of technology and succeeded in proving several points:

- With a critical mass of technology in a classroom, there could be a significant improvement in quality and effectiveness of instruction.
- With a team approach, teachers would more quickly assimilate technology as an instructional tool.
- Other schools would more easily become involved in the use of technology if there were a successful model in the system.
- Support from all levels of administration was necessary for such change to be successful.
- If properly approached, parents would be highly supportive of the enterprise.
- Students would find it natural and expect access to technology in their classrooms.

Recently the Wellesley, Massachusetts, Public Schools conducted a study with Boston College demonstrating that students
who were using AlphaSmarts (small, portable computers well-suited
for note taking on the fly) performed better on the Massachusetts
high-stakes student assessment tests when they used technology for
taking the tests than when they wrote long hand (Russell, 2000).

Technology in Its Place

It is important to emphasize that not everything a student learns in
school will be learned on the computer. Students will learn how to
write with a pen and pencil, how to read books, how to do calcula-
tions in their heads and on paper, how to solve problems by talking
and thinking them through, and how to be critical consumers of
information whatever the source. The key message to all stakeholders is the appropriate use of technology, not technology as a
panacea for all educational problems.

A related argument centers on the "computers versus teachers" dichotomy. The message must be that it is not a choice of one
or the other. Technology is a tool, albeit the most powerful tool a
teacher has ever possessed. Learning requires the personal interaction of two minds. It will be always be that way. Perhaps in the
future, schools will not look as they do now: a series of separate
"boxes" in a building. Technology has the potential to change the
structure of the school building and the timetable. Whatever
those look like in the future, though, there will be teachers working with children to facilitate their learning. But as we face a
future of teacher shortages, we must look for new and effective
ways in which the technology can help to compensate for this
great loss.

"Let the businesses teach technology later," say some oppo-
nents. "Why waste money on the schools?" Craig Moore (1998) at
the University of Massachusetts, Amherst has offered some valuable
insights on this question. The fact is that businesses are hungry for

entry-level and professional-level people right now. They want to hire trained people for their workforce, not provide basic training.

Student Safety and Appropriate Use

Schools must provide some protection against the objectionable use of computers both to satisfy parents that schools are safe and to ensure that valuable time is not wasted in school. Although it is true that the choice of books in a school library is screened by responsible adults and the Internet is not, schools can use filtering mechanisms, such as Internet proxy screening servers or desktop blocking software, and be reasonably sure that students are protected. (Chapter Ten provides a detailed discussion of this issue.)

Technical Support and Keeping Current

Schools must provide technical and support personnel. Teachers cannot stop teaching to fix equipment. If that is the case, they will stop using the technology—a reality often overlooked in schools. (It is never overlooked in business, where the information management service personnel ratio to computers is astronomical compared to a school district of similar size.) In our district (Acton), for forty-six hundred students in seven schools, we have a director of technology, two integration specialists, a network manager, and a supervisor of special programs. We consider these five full-time positions to be less than the minimum requirements for a responsive and smoothly functioning technology program.

Hardware Disposal

It is no surprise that computers in schools do become old. Policies to ensure the swift disposal of outdated equipment must be implemented in schools, or the problem of storage, long a school complaint, will be exacerbated. There are agencies that collect old

computers and distribute them to those in less fortunate circum-
stances. Schools need to be able to let go of technology that has
outlived its usefulness.

Which Operating Platform?

Which platform a district should invest in is surely connected to
use and purpose, and the issue will probably be debated periodically.
Unfortunately, the fight is time-consuming and sometimes incen-
diary. The essential subtext is a comparison of the following costs
(now referred to as total cost of ownership): acquisition, installation, maintenance, ease of use, number of support personnel,
teacher training, and prior investment in software.

Conclusion

Reconciling stakeholder interests is a constant balancing act. New
strategies will be identified and developed. Making sure the various
publics understand what is happening in schools, why it is important that students and teachers use technology, and establishing
reliable sources of funding will always be challenging issues. It helps
to have a network, human and electronic, that connects community members so that every stakeholder can be involved in the dialogue. Not everyone will be convinced, but the future will show
how important technology is in the school.

References

Education Week/The Milken Exchange on Education Technology. *Technology Counts '98: Putting School Technology to the Test.* [http://www.edweek. org/sreports/tc98/tchome.html]. 1998.

Hezel Associates. *Educational Telecommunications and Distance Learning: The State-by-State Analysis, 1998–1999.* Syracuse, N.Y.: Hezel Associates, 1998.

Lowd, B. "The Technology Coordinator as Political Activist." In I. K. Zimmer- man and M. F. Hayes (eds.), *Beyond Technology: Learning with the Wired*

Curriculum. Wellesley, Mass.: Massachusetts Association for Supervision and Curriculum Development, 1998.

Moore, C. "Information Technology: The New Foundation." In L. Browne and C. Moore (eds.), *Massachusetts Benchmarks: The Quarterly Review of Economic News and Insight*. Amherst: University of Massachusetts/Federal Reserve Bank of Boston, 1998.

Papert, S. *Mindstorms: Children, Computers and Powerful Ideas*. New York: Basic Books, 1980.

U.S. Office of Technology Assessment. *Teachers and Technology: Making the Connection*. Washington, D.C.: U.S. Government Printing Office, 1995.

Russell, M. *It's Time to Upgrade: Tests and Administration Procedures for the New Millennium*. Washington, D.C.: U.S. Department of Education, 2000. [http:www.ed.gov/Technology/techconf/2000/russell_paper.html].

Wenglinsky, H. *Does It Compute? The Relationship Between Educational Technology and Student Achievement in Mathematics*. Princeton, N.J.: Educational Testing Service, 1998. [http://www.ets.org/research/pic/technolog.html].

Chapter Nine

Strategies for Creating Successful Corporate Partnerships

John Richards

> Effective partnerships to support technology
> integration in the curriculum should be anchored
> in open communication, multiparty commitment,
> and mutual respect, and a moral vision should
> unite all participants in a common recognition
> of purpose.

Successful school-business partnerships are built on an understanding of each other's needs and constraints, mutual respect and honesty, and projects that are beneficial for all involved (see http://partnersineducation.org). Schools are designed to prepare students for the world of work, teach them to use their minds well, and encourage them to be thoughtful citizens and decent human beings (Sizer and Sizer, 1999). Businesses are designed to make money. They seek partnerships with schools to build their brand, become good corporate citizens, or sell product. The first two reasons, done respectfully, fall within guidelines established by the National Education Association and Consumers Union (1995). The third, selling product, clearly does not, and there are many ways that the first two can become objectionable. Here I examine several partnerships in which I have been involved and draw some lessons for teachers and businesses.

It is a mistake to speak of "business" as if it were a single type of entity with a single motivation. Different kinds of businesses come to school partnerships for various reasons and with differing agendas:

- Businesses whose products are marketed directly to educational institutions (examples are Harcourt, the Learning Company, and the educational divisions of Apple, IBM, and Compaq)
- Businesses (including colleges and universities) whose main job is research (such as Harvard University, RAND, SRA, BBN, and the National Science Foundation)
- Businesses with a peripheral financial interest in the education market (such as Turner Broadcasting, AT&T, the *New York Times*, and the Coca-Cola Company)
- Businesses that are interested in education for ostensibly prosocial reasons (such as public licensure requirements, positive publicity, community building, and public perception improvement; examples are the cable television industry and the tobacco industry)
- Businesses that market soft drinks, junk food, toys, clothing, and similar products to students

Schools and businesses have many common interests that provide a natural foundation for partnerships. Schools need to prepare students for the workplace, and businesses need workers who are prepared not only in basic skills but in the higher-order thinking skills and problem solving that form the core of most new curricula. Schools are looking for project-centered curricula that provide a context for learning and use real-world applications that demonstrate the relevance of the skills that students are learning.

Businesses by their very nature use science, math, language arts, and all curriculum areas in an interdisciplinary way. Moreover, they need employees who have the requisite knowledge and skills. At first glance, school-business partnerships seem like a win-win situation, a perception that is heightened when one recognizes that schools need money and businesses have it to give. Businesses need student consumers, and schools provide a captive audience. In this seeming solution, however, lies the conflict of financial resources and ethics.

Schools are designed to create citizens who, among other things, are critical consumers. Schools are places where students need to feel safe, where they can take intellectual chances, and where they will not be exploited. Businesses are interested in consumer brand recognition for potential revenue growth. It is the nature of their world to identify and exploit marketing opportunities. Schools are a prime target since products allowed into the school receive implicit endorsement.

The school endorsement makes a statement that students hear loud and clear. Sizer and Sizer (1999) propose that explicit teaching is only part of the important messages that schools send. Implicit messages are equally important. Peeling paint, for example, suggests that the community does not value the school. By contrast, teachers who involve their students in personal authentic research indicate that inquiry is a lifelong endeavor. Consequently, when corporations enter schools, they have an important message to give: that education is important in this society. However, Molnar (1996) argues that most partnerships cross over the line and create unnecessary curriculum merely to introduce product. When businesses use the school market merely to deliver a commercial message, businesses and schools send a wrong signal: that students are valued only as consumers.

Building on Strengths

Partnerships work when partners acknowledge and honor respective areas of expertise. For example, businesses can, by their very nature, provide schools with real-world experiences. In a recent poll, 82 percent of students, ages nine to seventeen, agreed with the statement, "I wish I could learn more about 'real life' in school, not just subjects like math and science" (Nickelodeon and Yankelovich, 1999). Businesses naturally produce real-life materials that may be used in project-centered learning and can show the relevance of students' and teachers' school experiences.

Having teachers or students team with, or shadow, business mentors provides exposure to business environments. The Georgia Industrial Fellowships for Teachers (GIFT) program provides summer work experiences for teachers and helps them take new science and math perspectives, new knowledge, and new strategies back to their classrooms. (See http://www.ceismc.gatech.edu/ceismc/programs/gift/.)

Traps and Land Mines

School-business partnerships can fail for many reasons:

• *Commercialism and marketing*. Schools need to be free of direct marketing to students. Both Molnar (1996) and House (1998) have attacked in-school marketing to students and any attempts to set up schools and students as economic targets. The National Education Association and Consumers Union (1995) have produced guidelines regarding the use of marketing materials in schools.

• *Divergent perceptions of time*. Schools and businesses have vastly different senses of time. For the school, implementation usually requires a year's advance notice. Teachers plan their school year the previous May and June. Teachers are very conservative in adopting new materials and very loyal once they see that something works in the classroom. Businesses are often looking for quick implementation

• *Buy-in*. A perceived lack of school commitment is a caution to business. Businesses are looking for fundamental agreements on goals and purposes and are skeptical about requests that seem to be thinly disguised requests for money. Businesses are, and should be, looking for clear endorsement at all levels of the school administration. Staff turnover is an issue at both the school and the business. Both the school and the business clearly need champions, but buy-in is also needed at multiple institutional levels.

- *Mutually recognized need.* The "field of dreams" ("If we build it, they will come") trap occurs when a business tries to fit a pet project into a school without genuinely teaming with the school and learning what the school really wants or needs.
- *Ignorance of the education profession.* Businesspeople have been through school, and a danger is that they assume that their own thirteen years of experience in the K–12 educational system means that they understand the education profession.
- *Ignorance of business.* Different departments within the same business will have very different interests and demands. Within a corporation, education department, or foundation, community affairs, public relations, or marketing will be looking for very different benefits. Educators often see businesses as monoliths possessing singular, common goals.

Case Histories of School-Business Partnerships

I have been involved in many school-business partnerships from the business side and have selected three to examine: a research institution's efforts to restructure schools, the cable industry's decade-long effort to provide commercial-free cable programming to schools and the newest initiative to provide cable modems, and the CNN Student Bureau, a new initiative from CNN and Turner Learning that provides journalism expertise and an outlet for student work on CNN.

BBN and the Co-NECT Design

In 1989 the Educational Technologies Division of BBN, a Cambridge, Massachusetts, research firm, won a New American Schools Development Corporation grant to redesign the organizational structure of schools. Its Co-NECT design was one of eleven winners out of almost seven hundred applicants (Goldberg and Richards,

1996). Today Co-NECT (http://www.co-nect.com) is a successful and effective design, but in the first years mistakes were made. The design addressed almost every aspect of school operation and curriculum. The Co-NECT project sought two schools as partners to help with the design in year 1 and to implement it in year 2. The participating schools were promised equipment in the process of restructuring.

One of the schools was in a large urban district and deeply committed to a very effective two-way bilingual program. Into this environment, the Co-NECT design introduced radical school change involving technology, project-centered learning, authentic assessment, and new governance structures.

To implement Co-NECT successfully, the school needed to be committed to these changes and to the significant staff development such change required. But the Co-NECT changes interfered with the commitment to the two-way bilingual program. The partnership broke down, and after two years BBN withdrew from the school. Why did it break down?

BBN did not do its homework properly. It asked for a faculty vote and other ways to see if there was genuine support for the changes, but it was in a rush to get a grant and, once it was awarded, to begin work. If BBN had built in more time, it would have recognized that financial support, not the Co-NECT design, was driving this school's participation.

The school never bought into the design, but since it had little modern technology, it could not resist the offer of nearly $500,000 in equipment. This is a common problem because schools are typically underfunded. According to the National Education Association (1997), teachers spend on average over $400 annually of their own money to meet perceived student needs. Schools are always looking for sources of materials, technology, and volunteers.

Another problem was a shift in support. The main supporter, an assistant superintendent, left after one year, eliminating an important pillar of support. With this departure BBN lost the support of the central urban district administration. This was critical, for example, when it was struggling to figure out how to install a computer network and add sufficient electric power to the building. One day without warning, massive trucks and large numbers of workers showed up to install new windows and paint and fix up the building. BBN was never able to get the cooperation needed to install its network during the renovation. The central school administration did not support BBN's effort and made no efforts to inform it of any construction plan.

These two experiences encouraged adjustments to BBN's design and approach. One was never to promise equipment and infrastructure, particularly in the recruiting stage. Another was to seek support at several administrative levels.

The Co-NECT design endures and is an extremely successful model for partnership. It has been transformed over eight years by interaction with dozens of school systems and more than 115 schools. Among the changes is the development of an extensive memorandum of understanding, whereby the roles and responsibilities of each of the participants is set forth.

Cable in the Classroom

Cable in the Classroom, launched in 1989, is a public service effort supported by forty-one national cable networks and over eighty-five hundred local cable companies. These networks and local cable companies act as partners in learning with teachers and parents by providing a free cable connection and over 540 hours per month of commercial-free educational programming to schools.

Cable networks, such as CNN, Discovery, A&E, and Nickelodeon, set aside a portion of their schedule to air commercial-free programming on subjects as varied as science, art history, math, literature, and world events. Some of the programming is created specifically for a network's Cable in the Classroom offering (one is CNN's daily half-hour *CNN NEWSROOM* program); other networks, such as A&E, often reformat documentaries or other programs from their regular schedule into "teacher-friendly" modules.

All of the programs are copyright cleared for at least a year, so schools can build their own video libraries.

Local cable companies provide a cable connection into every school in their service areas. Teachers may record Cable in the Classroom programming at home or can ask their school's media coordinator or librarian to record programs on the school's video recorder. By videotaping a program, teachers can keep it and use it when it is convenient and fits into their curriculum.

Because Cable in the Classroom programming is commercial free and intended to be videotaped rather than used in real time, most programs air off-hours. A regular programming schedule and detailed program descriptions are available in *Cable in the Classroom* magazine and *Cable in the Classroom Online* (http://www. ciconline.org).

Cable in the Classroom fulfills schools' need for supplementary classroom materials and the cable industry's need to develop positive community relations. The value to the cable industry was made clear when the Federal Communications Commission (FCC) passed a ruling requiring three hours per week of educational programming from the broadcast networks. The FCC excluded cable networks because of their diversified educational offerings and their demonstrated commitment to Cable in the Classroom.

As part of a resolution of various disputes, most cable companies have entered into a social contract that now commits them to continue this effort and extend it to wiring schools with cable modems. This effort serves both the schools and the cable companies. Schools will get the infrastructure they require for cable and, with cable modems, the Internet.

CNN *Student Bureau*

In August 1989, Ted Turner launched *CNN NEWSROOM* (CNNNR), a cost-free, commercial-free news and features program designed specifically for classroom use, currently airing on CNN from 4:30 to 5:00 A.M. (U.S. Eastern Standard Time). CNNNR is designed to inform students and teachers about current events, provide materials designed to provide a broad, international perspective, and create a sense of global citizenry. It is currently used in more than twenty-three thousand schools around the world.

News creates a real-time challenge to teachers. They need to be prepared to lead a discussion on everything from school violence to bombings in Afghanistan. While CNNNR tries to give advance warning on features or "desk segments," breaking news is by its nature something for which everyone is unprepared. Turner Learning provides a daily teacher's guide (available at http://cnnfyi.com/NEWS ROOM/) with specific curriculum connections and discussion questions. For sensitive issues, such as school violence, particular care is taken to provide context and perspective. As a business-school partnership, Turner provides access to what CNN does best, and teachers are free to use whatever segments of the show they feel fit into their curriculum.

Turner Learning extended the initiative when it announced the CNN Student Bureau (CNNSB), a virtual student news source, distributed worldwide, that gives students an opportunity to be published and recognized by CNN. As the official student news-gathering and reporting bureau for CNN, CNNSB offers students an opportunity to be published on the Web, on CNNNR, and potentially on the broader CNN News Group. CNNSB gives students a forum to report the news from their perspective.

CNNSB puts authentic learning activities in students' hands so they understand how events affect their lives and define their roles in society, making them better global citizens. Covering and reporting news is an authentic, project-centered team activity that depends on multiple media for its products. The students' portfolios are the compilation of all of their contributions to the news products.

Participation in CNNSB is open to high schools and universities worldwide. As a high school program, CNNSB is integrated into journalism, English, history, and science departments, as an interdisciplinary program, or as a club. At the university level, CNNSB works with mass communication, journalism, and other areas interested in communicating news and information.

Schools and institutions designated as CNNSB sites receive print and multimedia materials, including CNN student reporter and production-style guidelines, curriculum guides, procedures, and access to CNN Newsource, a satellite feed of footage that schools can edit. The goal of CNNSB is to establish a standard by which future reporters and production staffs create, view, and report news (see http://turnerlearning.com/sb).

In one and a half years of operation, almost five hundred schools, from forty-nine states and thirty-five countries, are participating in CNNSB. It has aired more than sixty student-produced stories on the CNN networks. CNNSB is succeeding because it offers a natural challenge that demands a high quality of student work. The educational reward—students' creating something of recognized value—offers the authenticity that schools want. CNN benefits from access to the student voice and from participation in community building that accords with our corporate values.

Conclusion

Sizer and Sizer write, "We have a profound moral contract with our students. We insist under the law that they become thoughtful informed citizens. We must—for their benefit and ours—model such citizenship" (1999, p. xviii)

In its "Preserve Classroom Integrity Pledge," the National Education Association (Molnar, 1996, p. 186) states:

Any business program should:

- Have real educational value and promote a love of learning

- Reinforce basic classroom curricula, not contrived activities

- Advance an educational goal, not merely a public relations purpose

- Allow any decision to participate to be made at the school level
- Be open to students who voluntarily choose to participate

It should not:

- Offer trips, gifts, or prizes in exchange for teachers pushing commercial products in their classrooms
- Discriminate against any group of students
- Impede or interfere with student instructional time
- Require the purchase of a product by students or parents
- Require teachers, students, or parents to promote a commercial product

It is critical to establish a written agreement at the beginning of a project partnership in which each party honestly represents its wishes, desires, and obligations. In order to be effective, all parties must understand the reason behind the other parties' involvement. If they are in any way uncomfortable with this, the project terms needs to be renegotiated. Such partnerships absolutely rely on honest, full disclosure.

The school has a moral mission as well as an instructive one. It is critical that businesses take this into account in partnering with schools. Businesses have the power to give students the message that education is critically important and that society is committed to challenging and educating all of its citizens. Treating students simply as consumers and teachers as salespeople is an inappropriate strategy for effective collaboration.

References

Consumers Union. *Captive Kids: Commercial Pressures on Kids at School*. Yonkers, N.Y.: Consumers Union Education Services, 1995.

Goldberg, B., and Richards, J. *The Co-NECT Design for School Change*. In S. Stringfield (ed.), *The New Reform*. Baltimore, Md.: Johns Hopkins University Press, 1996.

House, E. R. *Schools for Sale*. New York: Teachers College Press, Columbia University, 1998.

Molnar, A. *Giving Kids the Business: The Commercialization of America's Schools*, Boulder, Colo.: Westview Press, 1996.

National Association of Partners in Education. Alexandria, Virginia. [http://partnersineducation.org].

National Education Association. *Status of the American Public School Teacher, 1995–96: Highlights*. Washington, D.C.: National Education Association, 1997. [http://www.nea.org/nr/status.pdf].

Nickelodeon and Yankelovich. *Youth Monitor, 1999 Trend Reference Book*. Norwalk, Conn.: Yankelovich Partners, 1999.

Sizer, T. R., and Sizer, N. F. *The Students Are Watching*. Boston: Beacon Press, 1999.

Chapter Ten

Using Technology Appropriately

Policy, Leadership, and Ethics

Linda de Lyon Friel

Responses to the issues surrounding information
ethics, policy development, and responsibility must
reflect the educational goals and expectations of
each school and school system.

Technology access and use raise difficult questions for educational
leaders about information ethics, policy development, and responsibility. But there are no prescriptive answers; one size does not fit all.

Although policy development is a local issue, the process is gen-
eric. It begins by researching, evaluating, and revising existing policies and then moves on to the work of writing the policy. Repman
and Downs (1999) highlight several policy decisions that must be
made: whether the policy should cover a single school or the district,
whether there should be different versions for students at different
grade levels, and the differences between a policy and a procedure.

Committees involving as many stakeholders as possible need to
convene to discuss and research the issues and then write and
review the draft. Once the draft is completed, it is a prudent idea to
have an attorney read it and provide feedback about any necessary
changes. The school board must then approve the policy in order
to give it teeth. Finally, staff must be apprised of the new policies
and any changes from the old policies. Once created, policies must
be reviewed and revised regularly in order to ensure that they are
current and meet school needs.

Information Literacy

Changing technologies result in ever-expanding information access and the need to evaluate and use that information appropriately. *Information Power: Building Partnerships for Learning* (American Association of School Librarians and Association for Educational Communications and Technology, 1998) states that "information literacy—the ability to find and use information—is the keystone of lifelong learning" (p. 1). The document focuses on the needs of students as they develop into lifelong learners, while emphasizing information, processes, and thinking skills. (The American Library Association *Information Power* home page can be found at: http:// www.ala.org/aasl/ip_toc.html.)

Information Power's standards provide schools with a ready-made structure through which leadership, ethics, and responsibility in technological environments can be exercised. The Information Literacy Standards for Student Learning address three broad areas: information literacy, independent learning, and social responsibility. Each standard has its own indicators and proficiency levels and is linked to subject areas.

Because the literacy standards are aligned with student learning standards from all subject areas, the library media program provides a vehicle to support and facilitate new ways to maximize student learning. "Busy classroom teachers concerned with implementing their own content area standards will be most receptive to information literacy guidelines when [library] media specialists show how information literacy can help students achieve success in content areas" (Anderson, 1999, p. 12).

Leadership of the Information Research Process

To achieve information literacy, students must learn to access, evaluate, and synthesize information and then put it to use. Neuman (1999) recognizes the gap between students' understandings of how information and ideas are organized and the ways in which this information is put together by designers of digital resources and Web pages. These students, however, "need guidance and intervention from the school's experts (teachers and library media specialists) at every step of their journey to information literacy" (p. 42).

Because educators have the responsibility to help students become critical and competent evaluators of information and independent, lifelong learners, educators must also provide leadership and a willingness to turn this vision into reality. One way of accomplishing this is through the teaching of the information research process to students within the context of subject area curricula. (See Chapter One.)

There are numerous research models (McGregor, 1999) that can be employed to help students make sense of information, and it does not matter which model is employed; all of them have proved their efficacy. What does matter, however, is the need for the collaboration of the entire school community and the infusion of the school culture with a student-based learning and problem-solving focus. All of the school staff must fully understand the school's goals, the skills and strategies that students must learn, the research model being used, and how student improvement and achievement will be assessed. Schmoker (1996) maintains that results occur only with teamwork, goals, and careful analysis and use of data.

Copyright Issues

Although the Internet and other technologies have proven to be valuable educational resources, their integration into classrooms presents legal questions that might differ from the more traditional copyright issues.

U.S. copyright law gives authors of original works of authorship (a work can include text, pictures, sounds, and other components) exclusive rights to that work as soon as it is put into fixed form. The work can be published or unpublished, with or without copyright notices. A safe and practical assumption is that all works are copyrighted. "Anytime you copy a work protected by copyright, there must be something that allows that copy to be made" (Loundy, 1999, p. 20). In this technological age, printing a document or saving it to a disk can be construed as making a copy.

U.S. copyright law (17 U.S. Code, section 107 [revised Feb. 1, 1993]) contains a fair use provision that allows copyrighted work to be used "for purposes such as criticism, comment, news reporting, teaching, . . . scholarship, or research." Four factors must be considered when defining fair use: the purpose and character of the use, the nature of the copyrighted work, the portion of the work used in relation to the work as a whole, and the effect of the use on the potential market for the work.

Many Web sites provide information about copyright issues, among them the following:

- Copyright Web site: http://www.benedict.com/
- Copyright basics from the U.S. Copyright Office, Library of Congress: http://lcweb.loc.gov/copyright/
- Stanford University Libraries, on copyright and fair use: http://fairuse.stanford.edu/
- Copyright for educators at James Madison University: http://falcon.jmu.edu/~ramseyil/copy.htm

Plagiarism

Today's technology allows students access to mountains of information, and this access can make it tempting and easy to appropriate information and then pass it off as original work. Students have plenty of opportunity and encouragement to cheat; many Web sites, for example, sell term papers.

Educators must teach students the importance of citing all of their sources, no matter what the format. E-mail, listservs, and newsgroups necessitate careful student documentation concerning the senders and the context in which the messages were sent or posted. The meaning of the messages and the senders' identities must be acknowledged.

McKenzie (1998) argues that educators who require students to prepare simple fact-finding research papers are encouraging those students to access only information; instead, students should be learning higher-level thinking skills such as evaluation and synthesis. Fact finding encourages students to copy and paste material from electronic sources—a new form of plagiarism. One possible solution to the "new plagiarism" is changing the way educators teach students to research and manage information. If students are taught to synthesize information and construct their own answers and meanings, the temptation to appropriate others' ideas as their own is minimized. The teaching of these higher-level skills must be tied to research across the curriculum. The library media specialist can coordinate the effort but cannot teach the skills alone and in isolation.

On-Line Citations

Once students are accessing on-line information and using it in their research and learning, the next step is to teach them proper citation form for electronic sources. Standard style manuals have been slow to respond to this need, and forms are still evolving (Ivey, 1997; LeBaron, Collier, and Friel, 1997). A style manual devoted exclusively to proper form for on-line citations is Li and Crane's *Electronic Styles: A Handbook for Citing Electronic Information* (1996). The most important thing to remember is that form should be consistent and allow the reader to locate the cited information (LeBaron, Collier, and Friel, 1997).

The following Web sites are useful for guidelines for on-line citations:

- Longman English Online Citation Guides: http://longman.awl.com/englishpages/

- Bibliographic formats for citing electronic information: http://www.uvm.edu/~ncrane/estyles/
- Internet Public Library: http://www.ipl.org/ref/QUE/FARQ/netciteFARQ.html
- Advice on citing on-line sources: http://www.quinion.com/words/articles/citation.htm

Information Policies

Information policies must be put together on several related issues: intellectual freedom, censorship, filters, acceptable use, privacy, and child safety.

Intellectual Freedom

Intellectual freedom, guaranteed by the First Amendment to the U.S. Constitution, allows freedom of expression and the freedom to access ideas and information without regard to the content or viewpoint of the author or the user (American Library Association, Office for Intellectual Freedom, 1996). It thus requires physical and intellectual access, and this access extends to resources outside the walls of the school and library media center.

Traditionally schools and media centers are expected to provide students with print and nonprint information in many formats, while protecting intellectual freedom. Two Web sites address intellectual freedom:

- Librarian Links: http://www.gwi.net/brhs/lib.html
- Washington Library Media Association Online: http://www.wlma.org/default.htm

The American Library Association (ALA) has developed a number of policies that address access and technology issues; among them are *Resolution on the Filtering of Software in Libraries*,

ALA Code of Ethics, *Library Bill of Rights*, *Free Access to Libraries for Minors*, *Access to Resources and Services in the School Library Media Program*, and *Access to Electronic Information*, *Services*, *and Networks*. (Many of these can be accessed from ALA's home page, at http://www.ala.org/, or from http://winslo.state.oh.us/publib/poliaddi.html.) It is important for school policy committees to discuss these philosophical and educational issues and then develop policies that reflect each school's unique vision and mission.

Censorship

The ALA and the Association for Educational Communications and Technology have come out strongly against restricting access to a variety of viewpoints in schools. At the same time, however, educators are aware that every school should have a materials selection and reconsideration policy that covers materials in all formats and reflects the school's goals and mission statement, its curriculum, and the needs of its students. Such a document should also specifically outline a process for dealing with challenged materials.

Not all information found on the Internet is appropriate, accurate, complete, reliable, or current. Because censorship is subjective, however, perhaps the best way to approach Internet use is to stress guidance rather than censorship (LeBaron, Collier, and Friel, 1997; McKenzie, 1995a). Educators can model informed and ethical use of the Internet and teach students to evaluate information and sites.

Schrock (1999) has developed twenty-six criteria for site evaluation that take authenticity, applicability, authorship, and usability into account. Library media specialists and teachers can integrate site evaluation into subject area curricula. In addition, Web sites that support the curriculum and provide developmentally appropriate information can be emphasized. Students can learn the responsible use of technology only when they try it themselves. The task of teaching students to use this technology responsibly falls jointly to library media specialists and teachers.

The following Web site provides a link to censorship information:

Librarian Links: http://www.gwi.net/brhs/lib.html

Internet Filters

Software programs are available that block sites containing objectionable material. The programs, however, can only distinguish technical file characteristics; they cannot make value judgments about a site's informational content. The result is that sites that are educationally viable may be blocked (McKenzie, 1999). In addition, objectionable sites sometimes move very quickly from one server to another. Often the manufacturers of these software programs will not release the lists of sites that are blocked; some sites may be blocked for political or other reasons. Finally, these filters can be expensive and require staff time for installation and updating (Johnson, 1998).

Each school must make its own decision concerning the use of blocking software. Some will have reservations about restricting free access of information; others will see the software as a legitimate way to regulate access to information that the school and the community might see as inappropriate. Because it is impossible to block everything that might be deemed objectionable, perhaps the best solution is to teach responsible Internet use and then give students the freedom to make informed and appropriate choices. Blocking software cannot substitute for education and supervision.

The following sites provide helpful information on filtering:

- "A Dozen Reasons Why Schools Should Avoid Filtering," at *From Now On*: http://fno.org/mar96/whynot.html
- Filtering the Internet in American Public Libraries: http://www.firstmonday.dk/issues/issue2_10/bastian/index.html

Acceptable Use Policies

Although the integration of technology into curricula provides expanded learning opportunities for students, it may also result in difficult situations—for example:

- A teacher reports receiving an obscene e-mail message.
- A staff member uses his or her e-mail account to run a personal business.
- Students share passwords and use one another's accounts.
- A student hacks into the network system, corrupts several files, and is caught.
- A student is found with sexually explicit material accessed through the school's Internet file server.

An acceptable use policy (AUP) for a school system sets the conditions under which the computer network may be used. A well-developed AUP should cover Internet and intranet use, outline the appropriate and ethical behaviors that are expected from users of the network, and provide consequences for policy violations. It must also be flexible enough to cover unforeseen situations.

A carefully developed and publicized AUP will leave no confusion about what the network rules are, will clearly delineate the school's expectations for computer network integration into the curriculum, and will also help to prevent cries of unfairness when violators suffer the consequences of their inappropriate computer use. Whenever possible, these consequences should be derived from existing disciplinary policies.

McKenzie (1995b) maintains that schools need board policies—that is, policies at the level of the school board. Board policies are broader in scope than AUPs and address educational and philosophical issues such as the need to link AUP standards to policies on student rights and responsibilities that the district might already have in place. A board policy also "takes a position on access to potentially controversial information and relates these new information sources to pre-existing policies on curriculum and the selection of curriculum materials, outlining clear expectations for staff supervising student use" (McKenzie, 1995a).

Following are some Web sites containing information and links to policies:

- Bellingham, Washington, Board Policy:
  http://www.bham.wednet.edu/policies.htm
- Armadillo at Rice University:
  http://chico.rice.edu/armadillo/Rice/Resources/accept able.html
- Internet Advocate:
  http://www.monroe.lib.in.us/~lchampel/netadv.html
- K–12 Acceptable Use Policies:
  http://www.erehwon.com/k12aup/

The development of an AUP can generate productive communication among staff, students, parents, and the larger community and can be a starting point for collaborative teaching and discussion of personal responsibility. "Using the Internet to conduct discussion on relevant issues (such as plagiarism, obscenity, racism, information evaluation, and data theft) can involve students, teachers, and parents in the construction of their own awareness and values about the issues involved" (LeBaron, Collier, and Friel, 1997, pp. 85–86).

Privacy Issues

When a student sends e-mail, usually there are myriad opportunities for people other than the addressee to read, make a copy of, or change it. Although educators are expected to address privacy issues when they teach students about Internet and e-mail use, there is no law and no way that network users can be guaranteed absolute privacy in their telecommunications. Educators should structure as much electronic privacy as possible.

At the same time, students should be apprised that the school assumes responsibility for its own electronic equipment. As with student lockers, the computer equipment is school property and can be searched without a search warrant if school cfficials have reasonable cause to suspect inappropriate use. The best way to maintain as much privacy as possible is to have a well-written AUP in place that is included in the yearly student handbook.

The following site provides numerous links to privacy issues in education:

SafeKids.com: http://www.safekids.com/index.htm

Child Safety

Although most Internet experiences are positive, there have been a number of well-publicized incidents where children have been victimized or exploited by on-line criminals. To ensure student safety, it is not enough to regulate and monitor student access. Schools must make students, teachers, and parents aware of potential dangers and safety precautions. Awareness building can help to protect students and also help build parent support for the integration of technology into the student learning experience.

Here are two Internet safety sites:

SafeKids.com: http://www.safekids.com/index.htm
Sofweb's Taking Care on the Internet:
    http://www.sofweb.vic.edu.au/internet/takecare.htm

Conclusion

Technology adds a twist to the jobs of educators and necessitates some important problem solving. The solutions to the problems, however, must evolve through the collaborative efforts of stakeholders. Thoughtful discussion and reflection are required, and differing viewpoints and philosophies must be addressed. The solutions must reflect the educational goals and expectations of each school and school system.

References

American Association of School Librarians and Association for Educational Communications and Technology. *Information Power: Building Partnerships for Learning*. Chicago: American Library Association/Washington, D.C.: Association for Educational Communications and Technology, 1998.

American Library Association, Office for Intellectual Freedom. *Intellectual Freedom Manual*. (5th ed.) Chicago: American Library Association, 1996.

Anderson, M. A. "Creating the Link: Aligning National and State Standards." *Book Report*, 1999, *17*(5), 12–14.

Ivey, K. C. "Untangling the Web: Citing Internet Sources." *Editorial Eye*. [http://www.eeicom.com/eye/utw/96aug.html]. 1997.

Johnson, D. "Internet Filters: Censorship by Any Other Name?" *Emergency Librarian*, 1998, *25*(5), 11–13.

LeBaron, J., Collier, C., and Friel, L. D. *A Travel Agent in Cyber School: The Internet and the Library Media Program*. Englewood, Colo.: Libraries Unlimited, 1997.

Li, X., and Crane, N. B. *Electronic Styles: A Handbook for Citing Electronic Information*. (Rev. ed.) Medford, N.J.: Information Today, 1996.

Loundy, D. "New User Basics—Student Content and Copyright Law: Separating Fact from Fiction." *Classroom Connect*, 1999, *5*(5), 20–21.

McGregor, J. "Teaching the Research Process: Helping Students Become Lifelong Learners." *NASSP Bulletin*, 1999, *83*(605), 27–34.

McKenzie, J. "Protecting Our Children from the Internet (and the World)." *From Now On*, 1995a, *4*(10). [http://www.fno.org/fnojun95.html].

McKenzie, J. "Creating Board Policies for Student Use of the Internet." *From Now On*, 1995b, *5*(7). [http://www.fno.org/fnomay95.html].

McKenzie, J. "The New Plagiarism: Seven Antidotes to Prevent Highway Robbery in an Electronic Age." *From Now On*, 1998, *7*(8). [http://www.fno.org/may98/cov98may.html].

McKenzie, J. "Since When Is Adult a Dirty Word?" *From Now On*, 1999, *8*(8). [http://fno.org/may99/adult.html].

Neuman, D. "What Do We Do After the School Has Been Wired? Providing Intellectual Access to Digital Resources." *NASSP Bulletin*, 1999, *83*(605), 35–43.

Repman, J., and Downs, E. "Policy Issues for the Twenty-First Century Library Media Center." *Book Report*, 1999, *17*(5), 8–11.

Schmoker, M. *Results: The Key to Continuous School Improvement*. Alexandria, Va.: Association for Supervision and Curriculum Development, 1996.

Schrock, K. "The ABCs of Web Site Evaluation." *Classroom Connect*, 1999, *5*(4), 4–6.

Index